From the
Blitz to the Burmese Jungle and Beyond

A Memoir by
Brian Hennessy

with Karen McMillan

A catalogue record for this e-book is available from the National Library of New Zealand.

ISBN: 978-0-473-37431-0

Text © Karen McMillan 2017
The moral rights of the author have been asserted.
Design and format © McKenzie Publishing 2017

All rights reserved. No part of this publication may be reproduced, stored in a retrieval system, or transmitted in any form or by any means, without permission in writing from the publisher, nor be otherwise circulated in any form.

Designed by CVD Limited (www.cvdgraphics.nz)
International distribution: Ingram Spark (Lightning Source)

'S/S/T Hennessy is hardworking and efficient. Note he is most reliable and has shown a strong sense of responsibility. Absolutely trustworthy and sober.'

—W. Y. Dunnett, September 5, 1946

'I was solely responsible for the maintenance of all instruments issued to the 26,000 men of the 29th Assault Brigade, the 72nd Assault Brigade, 26th Brigade, 5th Brigade, 2nd and 36th Divisions in Burma …'

—Brian Hennessy, in a letter
written shortly after the war

Contents

Prologue   11

1.	Cologne, Dover and London	*Dec 1921 – Aug 1939*	13
2.	London	*Sep 1939 – Jun 1941*	19
3.	Mill Hill, Bury and York	*Jun 1941 – May 1943*	27
4.	Durban and Bombay	*Mar – Jun 1943*	35
5.	Allahabad	*Jul 1943*	41
6.	Nira	*Aug 1943*	45
7.	Madh Island	*Aug 1943*	51
8.	Ahmednagar	*Sep 1943*	55
9.	Poona	*Oct 1943*	63
10.	Nashik	*Nov 1943*	73
11.	Bawli Bazaar	*Feb 1944*	77
12.	Buthidaung	*Feb 1944*	81
13.	Buthidaung	*Mar 1944*	91
14.	Buthidaung	*Apr 1944*	97
15.	Shillong	*May – Jul 1944*	101
16.	Tinsukia	*Aug 1944*	107
17.	Digboi and Samaw	*Sep 1944*	111
18.	Samaw	*Sept 1944*	119

19. Myitkyina	*Oct 1944*	*125*
20. Hopin	*Nov 1944*	*131*
21. Naba, Tinsukia and Shillong	*Dec 1944*	*137*
22. Katha	*Jan 1945*	*141*
23. Bahe	*Feb 1945*	*145*
24. Bahe and Mongmit	*Mar 1945*	*151*
25. Mong Long and Mandalay	*Apr 1945*	*157*
26. Meiktila	*May 1945*	*161*
27. Poona, Rangoon and Nashik	*Jun – Sep 1945*	*165*
28. Nashik and Bombay	*Oct 1945 – Mar 1946*	*169*
29. Kure and Hiroshima	*Apr – Jun 1946*	*171*

Final tribute   *179*
About the authors   *184*

Prologue

I sought cover behind a fallen tree, my fishing rod discarded by the side of the Burmese river. The firing was coming from across the river, bullets ricocheting into the ground in front of me and into the tree that I crouched behind, the Japanese unrelenting in their attempts to kill me.

My heart was racing. My shirt had stuck to my back in the tropical heat and my stomach growled, not so much from fear but from hunger. I glanced behind me, but the bank was too steep to make an escape. I considered firing back, but that would only give my position away, and what good would my Sten gun do when I was outnumbered like this anyway?

My only option was to remain crouched behind the fallen tree, alone and many thousands of miles from home. Was this how my life was going to end? I looked around me at the fast-flowing river, at the dense vegetation, alive with insects, and then up at the sky, blue and clear. It seemed too beautiful a day to die. I vowed today would not be that day.

Chapter 1
Cologne, Dover and London
Dec 1921 – Aug 1939

I was born in Cologne, Germany, to English parents on December 10, 1921. My father was a British soldier, and he had a caretaker post in Germany after World War One. I come from an army family. My grandfather was also in the army, and his father before him. In fact, our family's armed service dates back to 1715. You could say that I was born in the army, I grew up in the army and then I served in the army for many years.

You may have heard of Hennessy cognac. An ancestor, James Hennessy, was a captain in the Irish Brigade. They were called the Wild Geese. They were soldiers who left Ireland to serve in European armies, but I think the name came about because they made so much noise! There was a battle long ago in which France was being attacked by the Austrians. Even though the Austrians had fewer troops, the French were losing the battle. The King of France asked the Wild Geese to come quickly and save them from losing Paris. They travelled thirty miles and instead of resting they went straight into the thick of battle. They caused so much havoc the Austrians were forced to retreat and the King was so pleased that he gave a vineyard to my ancestor. James Hennessy married a Frenchwoman and her father invented what we now know as cognac brandy. It proved to be very popular in France, and they also sent it back to Ireland.

I was only a young boy when I was injured, and I spent many months in a military hospital recovering. I am too young to remember much, but, according to my parents, some children released the brakes on my pram. I was at the top of the hill and was badly hurt when the pram finally came to a stop. But despite being injured and having frequent periods in hospital for many years as a child, I think that experience ultimately shaped my life in a positive way. I learnt a lot about patience when I was in hospital. They had the most wonderful, beautifully made toys in Germany, so if they got bent or damaged, I would straighten them and repair them. My mother used to help in the kitchen, so I got passed around the hospital a fair bit. I got used to being with other adults, rather than just my parents, and I think that was a good thing for me too.

I always had a love of nature. When I was out of hospital, I enjoyed breeding newts. I thought they were utterly fascinating. The females were dark on top with orange and black dots underneath, while the males were a pale green colour. They used to lay eggs in the water plants, rolling the leaves up to protect them. When they hatched, they looked a little like tadpoles. When these amphibians matured, they had a lizard-like body, although they were semi-aquatic. Through a child's eyes, they were astonishing to observe.

We moved to England when I was about six years old, and my father was stationed at Dover Castle. My mother was pregnant with my younger brother, and there was an army hospital nearby. Father and his team were responsible for the horses for special occasions, the ones that pulled carriages and wagons. He was always very good with horses, and he used to spend hours polishing the harness brasses to ensure they were perfect. He was also a welterweight boxing champion in the army. He certainly didn't believe in mollycoddling, and I was taught to never show that I was in pain if I was hurt. My father was a very popular man in the army. He used to sing and dance, and he played the mandolin beautifully. He'd found a mandolin in new condition in the German trenches of the First World War that he used to play.

When I was a child, we regularly had colonels and majors in our house, and I learnt from them what it really meant to be an officer in the army. However, I decided I didn't want to join the army when I grew up. I didn't want to end up in a role where I would be ordering other men around. I think it was a bit of a disappointment to my father that I didn't want to have anything to do with the army – I wanted to pursue a technical career. I only joined because war broke out.

My mother was a wonderful woman. Before she married, she worked as a milliner on Oxford Street – which meant she was really good at what she did. She was clever and a very good artist. She fed not only our family but also my uncle's family, because my father's brother was sometimes unemployed. This was in the days before refrigerators, when they used to keep produce on ice. My mother used to wait until the last bus had left the village, buy up the meat, fish and cheese that they sold off cheaply at the end of the day and then walk for miles home with enough food to feed two families. To begin with, she had a string bag that used to cut through her fingers. When I was ten, I made a cloth bag for her with handles, with help from a teacher at school. I still have it, even though it has been washed so many times the pattern has faded away.

My sister, Doreen, was only a year younger than me, and we were very close. She used to go to dance classes, and it was my job to look after her. She was the most beautiful girl in the village. I didn't have as much to do with my younger brother, Lionel, however, just because of the age difference.

At school, I was good at art and drawing, and I knew a lot about nature – so much so that the teachers would come to me for information – but otherwise I was a very ordinary student. I used to come up with the correct answers for mathematics, but I never showed any workings, so that always got me into trouble with the teachers. I wasn't very interested in English, geography or history either – so overall I wasn't very excited about school.

I wasn't a sporty boy. I played hockey, but I wasn't interested in other sports. I think one of the reasons I wasn't keen was that I had spent all of that time in hospital and hadn't played much physically when I was young. I had scars around my neck, and I still had to go into hospital quite regularly, so that impacted on what I was able to do.

But I did enjoy building things in my spare time, and I really enjoyed constructing model aircraft. I used to enter all the competitions for model planes, and I often won awards. One time, I made a model plane that flew from Southern England to Lincolnshire. I got it back six months later because I had written my name in large letters all over it. It had been found in a forest range, covered in silt.

Near where we lived was an airfield. My brother and I used to sit on our roof and watch the planes taking off and landing.

Cologne, Dover and London   *Dec 1921 – Aug 1939*

One day, we watched what I now believe was an early-model Hawker Hurricane coming in to land. It was coming in much too fast. It crashed through a fence into the army cricket grounds, where men were in the middle of a game. Needless to say, the men scattered in all directions, but when the plane finally came to rest, it had tipped over, and the pilot was dangling outside the plane by his straps. Several men cut him down and caught him when he dropped. We watched him say a few words to his rescuers, and then he walked back onto the airfield, got into another plane and took off again!

I used to go and see the men who were maintaining the aircraft, and they would teach me things about the planes. It was fascinating! I didn't dream about flying the planes, though. Instead, I used to think of the best ways to build and fix them. I'm pretty sure I could have built a full-size aircraft if I had wanted to, but mostly you wouldn't be allowed and they wouldn't let you fly them. There were also small aircraft factories opposite our house, and I used to go and learn as much as I could from the people there.

We moved close to London when I was a teenager, and I was so interested in repairing mechanisms that, when I was thirteen, I made myself a small workshop in our house, saved up money for some tools and started repairing instruments. I used to fix motorcar, truck and cycle speedometers. If anyone asked me if I could repair something, I told them I could. I learnt to work on all sorts of things. I didn't charge any money – I just did it because I enjoyed doing it. I repaired my mother's sewing machine, clocks and kitchen things, so I know she always relied on me for this. My mother's sewing machine needed to be completely dismantled to remove dried lubricant one time. I boiled parts clean and reassembled it using the best oil. Afterwards, the sewing machine was like new. Everything was quite easy for me in this regard.

I wasn't to know, but my interest in repairing things from a young age would shape my life, and also my experience of war, when I was older.

Chapter 2
London
Sep 1939 – Jun 1941

I was seventeen years old and a student at the Twickenham College of Arts when war broke out. It impacted on my life fairly quickly, because our school was immediately closed, but a conversation with a neighbour would have a more dramatic influence on my immediate future.

I was very keen to work for an instrument-engineering firm. Mr Garner lived up the road, and I talked to him one day about my ambitions. His daughter and my sister were best friends, and the conversation turned to all the repair work I was doing in my workshop, with my mother proudly mentioning all the things I had fixed.

'You'll never get qualified unless you work for a company that is registered,' he said. 'You're doing good work here, but it will never be recognised.'

We were sitting in our kitchen drinking tea when this topic came up – my sister and her friend had gone out to do some shopping, and my mother was baking.

'So what should I do?' I asked eagerly. His opinion was one I valued. He was an accountant at the Sperry Gyroscope Company, which was then one of the most prestigious instrument manufacturers in England and America.

He considered me for a moment before answering. 'Why don't you come along to our factory tomorrow, and I'll see what I can do to help?' he suggested with a smile.

I felt like I had been given a big, shiny gift, and I eagerly met him at the agreed time the next morning. He introduced me to some of the other workers and then asked me to go into a storeroom separate from the main factory. It was a typical storeroom, with rows of trays with all manner of parts in them. Each tray had a job card that detailed what needed to be done in the next stage of manufacturing.

'Pick a tray and do whatever it instructs,' said my neighbour. 'I'll come back a little later with the foreman, and we'll see how you've got on.'

Mr Garner walked to the door and then turned before leaving. 'We'll see if we like what you've done. Let's see if it's good enough and if you have the ability to work here.'

I eagerly started work on the first tray. It contained some parts from a code machine that needed to be put together. When I had finished, I looked at the door and saw that no one had returned, so I thought I might as well do another tray, this time working on a predictor, an anti-aircraft fire-control instrument. Still, no one came to check on me, so I continued to work on more trays until I had worked on every tray in the room. They were all very easy jobs. I did much more complicated work in my workshop at home. All I needed was plenty of common sense.

Eventually, I went looking for someone and found a woman in an office who was typing.

'Do you know where the foreman is? I asked.

'He's busy at the moment,' she replied.

'But what do I do with all these cards?' I asked, showing her the stack of cards that I had accumulated.

She snatched them from me and scowled. 'What are you doing with these? Who did this work?'

'I did,' I replied. I was sure I had done a good job, so I wasn't worried about answering her question.

She glared at me. 'Tell me who really did this or I'll fetch the foreman,' she said.

'I did tell you. I did it.'

'You wait right here,' she said.

She stomped from the office, returning moments later with a large man who was clearly the foreman. He frogmarched me to the room where I had done the work and began looking at all the instruments, examining them all closely.

'Did you do this work?' he asked.

'I did.'

He frowned at me. 'And you had no help?' he asked.

'No, I did this myself.'

I quickly found myself in the main factory, where about fifty people were busy working. Each was asked if they had done any work in the other room, and each reply came back in the negative. No one had been in that room that day. Soon, the scene became more chaotic, with people talking back and forth. That's when a union representative entered the factory area.

'He's got to go,' the man said, pointing at me. 'We're not having him in this workshop!'

'But what have I done wrong?' I asked, feeling confused and perplexed.

'I'm very sorry, but I'm going to have to ask you to leave,' said the union representative, escorting me from the area.

At that point, Mr Garner came rushing towards us, and he and the union man had a short, tense conversation. I soon learnt that in less than a day, I had done more than a week's work, and the union was upset.

'They will all go on strike if he stays,' the union representative was saying. 'Everyone feels like they are working hard enough without some talented upstart getting management thinking the staff should be working harder.'

They walked away from me, and I didn't hear the rest of the conversation, but soon the union man disappeared, shaking his head as he left, and Mr Garner turned to me.

'I'd like you to come with me to the main office building,' he said.

His face was so serious that I thought I was in trouble – that doing all that work was somehow a bad thing.

When we arrived at an adjoining building, I was greeted by a man who introduced himself as one of the senior management team.

'Sit down,' he said.

I suddenly wondered if they were going to arrest me. Was I in that much trouble for finishing off the instruments? Should I have only stuck to the one tray?

'We are very impressed with your work today,' he said with a smile, and my tension dissolved. 'We'd like to offer you a job as a production manager.'

It didn't take me long to answer. 'I'd like that very much.'

'Your work today has caused a bit of a ruckus with the union,' he said, raising his eyebrows. 'But we can offer you this position in a different area. I take it that won't be a problem?'

'No, not at all!'

I couldn't believe my luck – I would be working for one of the finest precision-instrument-engineering firms in the world. I still look back on my time with the Sperry Gyroscope Company very fondly. I was working with all the new technology of the time. We manufactured predictors and also copies of the Enigma German code machines and our own British code machines.

It was a demanding, full-time job, and I worked with about fifty others. The company was behind on its government contracts, so everyone was working extra hard to catch up. I was involved in inspecting the work, and I made sure that everything was up to scratch. If something wasn't up to standard, I corrected it. I didn't ask permission; I just got on and did the job. There was a lot of red tape at the time, so I did my best to fast-track things, and I liked seeing if I could improve the designs too. I didn't mention this to anyone, however, as I'm sure it would have got me into trouble for deviating from what was standard, even though I was making improvements!

I mainly used to work with predictors, which were one of the most complicated of the instruments at the time. The predictors used to forecast where enemy planes would be in about one minute's time. It took two men to operate them. They were one of my favourite instruments.

I also worked on flash spotters, which were instruments that measured the angle of a bomb flash through a pair of binoculars. Three people would note the angle from the north, and then they would cross the angles and know within inches where that particular bomb had gone off. This was useful because they could direct firemen to the correct location.

I didn't mind how many hours I worked, even if I had to

work through the night. I prided myself in making sure that when I was finished, everything was neat and tidy – whereas I sometimes saw other instruments with cigarette ends and other rubbish inside. I really enjoyed what I was doing.

When it came to the code machines, I thought the German and English ones we made at Sperry's were much nicer and more modern-looking than the actual German-built ones. They were quite complicated, however. They looked like typewriters but had a set of drums inside. You needed a code book, and you rotated the drums according to the message in the book. The code came out in groups of five letters, then another five letters, etc. We didn't see many finished codes, because they were keeping everything as hush hush as they could, but the few finished messages I saw were very short.

I always found it easy to work with the code machines, and I think part of that was due to my interest in complex watches. Before the war began, I had a number of very fine Swiss watches, which not only told the time but also had information about the sun and moon – and I used to enjoy taking them to pieces, cleaning them and putting them back together. I think that was good practice for the work I ended up doing in the war.

A year after the war started in Europe, we felt the effects of war in London when the Blitz began. Sperry's was based near West London, which wasn't as badly damaged as other areas, but it was still a terrible time. I volunteered and became a 'roof-spotter' at Sperry's in their main building. My job was to stand on the roof and decide if the aircraft overhead was German or ours. My task was to shout down my advice to another person by the stairs if people needed to go to the shelter.

Oddly enough, I wasn't concerned about getting hurt. I think my father caused me to react like this, because he always told me, 'Never show fear.' In his boxing matches, even if he was getting hurt, he would always laugh, and, in this way, he fooled his opponents into thinking they couldn't win. He often won a match with this tactic, even though he had been losing. I've never boxed – I don't think punching people is a very good idea – but I certainly didn't show fear when I was roof-spotting.

There were a number of hairy moments, of course. I was out one day on the roof, looking at the sky, when I saw two German dive-bombers coming towards us. They circled around several times. I raised the alarm and noted with almost casual indifference that when they dived, one after the other, they looked like they were coming straight for us. But when they got to the place where they should have released the bombs, they didn't. Instead, they flew on and dropped the bombs on a wooded area where there were no buildings at all. I still wonder if they had some fault with their technology or if the individuals weren't keen on bombing us for their own personal reasons.

Next to us, another company wasn't so lucky next time. The Firestone Tire and Rubber Company received a direct hit one afternoon. It is hard to describe the carnage this bomb created. The smell of burning rubber was utterly overpowering. I remember looking down from my vantage point through all the smoke at the huge hole in the roof and seeing all the firemen battling to put the blaze out. It was a surreal scene, but the thing that struck me most was that their clock had stopped at one o'clock, the time of impact.

Behind Sperry's, there were some old wooden houses that mainly belonged to elderly people. Away from work, I was also a volunteer fireman, and I discovered I was good at putting out incendiary bombs when they fell in these houses. There were several ways of doing this. One was to pour sand over them; another way was to spray water in the air above them. So long as they couldn't get oxygen, they couldn't work. If you knew what you were doing, it wasn't particularly dangerous. These incendiary bombs weren't very big, and they broke up into pieces on impact, pieces that were about as thick as my thumb and the length of an average pencil, but they were heavy enough to break through the tiled roofs of houses, which meant attics would soon be burning furiously. Because I was a small, wiry lad, I was able to get into these confined spaces, whereas most of the firemen were too big to fit. I would often get into an attic and the bombs would be over part of the floor. But I didn't get nervous – I was too interested to be afraid. I was fairly agile in those days, so I would just get in, do the job and get out again.

Of course, sometimes I ended up spending time in shelters. The one we had was quite effective and was made of solid concrete. There was room for six people, and the old ladies of the area often used to join us. Being prepared for any eventuality, I had an air rifle at home that I used to keep in perfect condition. We had the body of an ambulance from World War One in the bottom of our garden. I put a box of sand in the ambulance with rows of pins that I used for target practice. I had wonderful eyesight back then and was an excellent shot.

The ironic thing at this time was that we received some food parcels from Germany. Boxes filled with German sausages arrived via Spain. We never found out who sent them, but clearly some of our friends in Germany thought we were in need of supplies!

Chapter 3
Mill Hill, Bury and York
Jun 1941 – May 1943

In June 1941, I enlisted in the army. I didn't need to enlist, as my job was a reserved occupation, but I wanted to see something of the world, so that was my main motivation for joining up.

I was posted to the Marine Barracks in Woolwich, and first of all I had to do the basic training. The accommodation was pretty rough. We were housed in rooms with bare stone walls, and all the windows had been blown out by bombs. It seemed to rain all the time I was there, and it was bitterly cold. I found it tough going physically. The training was really rigorous, and I used to collapse onto the straw mattress that served as my bed utterly worn out at the end of each day.

Basic training took about three months, and for me it was mostly a miserable time. I was skinny, I found my tin helmet heavy and uncomfortable and firing my rifle gave me some nasty bruises, so I ended up putting padding under my shirt to prevent further injury. But worse yet, the chief instructor was a physical bully and clearly enjoyed picking on me. He was a gorilla of a man, tall, muscular and imposing, and he used to do things like throw sixty-pound bags of sand at us, which we were supposed to catch. He was also determined that I had to touch my toes. But despite being agile, I just couldn't do this – I was about six inches short, and he made my life a misery because of this. He used to jump on my back and try to force me to reach my toes. It is a miracle he didn't break my back.

A month into my training, I woke up feeling extremely ill. I had a blinding headache, my neck felt strangely stiff and my vision was blurry.

'I need to report in sick,' I told the men I was bunking with.

'To do that you need to go to the doctor's medical room,' one of the men told me.

'But I feel too unwell to even get up,' I said.

'They won't allow doctors to come here,' he said. 'You have to go to them.'

With the help of several of them, I got myself out of bed, but when I got to where the medical rooms were, I thought it must be some perverted joke. The medical rooms were at the top of a flight of very steep stairs. Climbing up these stairs felt like climbing up an Egyptian pyramid. At times, I had to resort to climbing on my hands and knees, but I finally got to the top and entered the medical room.

Inside the room there was a doctor, who eyed me coldly.

'I need to report in sick,' I said, expecting some sympathy from a medical professional.

'Well, if you can get up those stairs, there is clearly nothing wrong with you,' he snapped. 'I'm getting sick of you men faking illnesses to get time off.'

I was astonished. 'But I feel really unwell.'

'What are your symptoms?'

I was partway through listing them when the phone rang.

Mill Hill, Bury and York   Jun 1941 – May 1943

The doctor took the call, his expression changing as he listened to the caller. He now looked at me with obvious concern.

When he had finished the call, he took my temperature and shook his head when he saw how high it was.

'We need to get you to the hospital,' he said.

'Hospital?' I had only been expecting to have a day where I could crawl back into bed, not anything more.

'I think you might have meningitis,' he said.

I didn't have meningitis, but I did spend two weeks in the Royal Herbert Hospital recovering from a viral infection. After weeks of bad treatment, I was treated very well when I was there. The matron was an older woman who had nursed during the First World War, and she didn't put up with any nonsense from the young doctors. And I had a lovely young nurse who was a distant relation of the Queen and who made everyone smile. She drove a red sports car, which she seemed to have plenty of petrol for despite the rationing, and she was as personable as she was good-looking.

My father came to visit me while I was there, and, when he stopped by, he discovered that the colonel in charge of the hospital was an old friend of his. The colonel gave me three weeks' holiday when I was discharged, so I was fully well again before I had to complete the basic training.

After training, I spent some time in Darby doing general duties, and, in November 1941, my rank was upgraded to instrument mechanic. On my twentieth birthday, I was posted to a workshop in Colchester, in North East England.

When I first arrived there, the sergeant major who was in charge gave me a big box full of spare typewriter parts.

'Make me a typewriter that works,' he said.

I immediately saw this as an intellectual challenge. It was clear that this was going to be a difficult task, so I sorted through the box and grouped all the parts by manufacture. There were marginally more parts for one brand of typewriter, so I got their manufacturer's style guide and got to work. I put together what I could and then adapted the other pieces for what was missing. Soon I had a typewriter with all the type lined up. I took it to the sergeant major.

'The typewriter you requested, sir,' I said.

He had been sitting at his desk, and he looked up with a curious expression when I put the typewriter on his desk. He studied the machine and then looked at me.

'Don't you realise I give that box to everyone as a joke?' he asked, smiling. 'Nobody has ever put together a typewriter before. Well done, Hennessy!'

He was a technically minded man, and when he had to do his report, he gave me a really high rating. Thanks to him, I was transferred to the workshop at Mill Hill in February 1942.

Mill Hill was a workshop for brighter technical people. It was a manufacturing army workshop, and while I was there, I became classified as an A1 instrument mechanic. I made friends there with twin brothers who were originally from Germany. They were image carvers for the Catholic Church, and their entire family had emigrated to England years before when Hitler came into power and things became difficult for them. They were both exceptionally bright, and I found it interesting that whenever they did tests, they did all the work separately from each other but always achieved identical marks.

One time when I was at Mill Hill, I had to work on forty predictors that were later sent to North Africa. I had modified

Mill Hill, Bury and York Jun 1941 – May 1943

the design to be more accurate, so when the bombs exploded they would be closer to the plane. I saw a documentary on TV recently that claimed that in North Africa they shot down more German planes than anywhere else, so if that is correct, that was my work!

After passing numerous tests and courses, I was selected for training for armament artificer instruments at the Military College of Science in Bury, and I was posted there in April 1942. Normally you would have to be older than twenty-one to do this course, but they accepted me despite being underage because of my high marks. The ratio of armament artificer instruments to recruits selected for technical training was about one to eight hundred at that time, so I was extremely pleased to have this opportunity. Normally this would have been a three-year course, but because of the war and all the technical people they had lost at Dunkirk, the course was compressed into about seven months. It was hard work, and I spent all my time studying, but I felt it was worth it. I wasn't distracted by anything else. I didn't drink (I've never touched a drop in my life) and I didn't go out partying – I simply devoted myself to my studies.

The Royal Military College of Science was housed in a private property at that time, and the building was surrounded by tall trees. There were a lot of bedrooms and we shared two to a room. All the teachers were qualified professors and were very demanding, but I didn't mind this as I was learning so much. My handwriting at high speed wasn't very legible, so I used to write my first round of notes in the lectures, rewrite my notes again to be more legible and then rewrite everything again for the third time as neatly as I could with sketches and drawings. I got very high marks, so this approach clearly worked for me. On graduating, I became the youngest armament artificer in the army.

In October I was transferred to York. I worked there as an instrument mechanic, and I was kept very busy in their workshop. There were about twenty-five of us, and we repaired army truck speedometers and did other basic army repair work.

It was while I was in York that I befriended some Jewish people from Germany. They had fled the country, somehow travelled across the channel and were caught and arrested when they arrived before eventually finding work. Most couldn't speak English, and the ones I met repaired trucks. Of course, I still spoke German from my early years growing up there, so I struck up conversations with them. I felt so sorry for them – many of them had lost all their families, although not many of them wanted to talk about their experiences. But when they did talk, the stories were horrifying. One man I met had been involved in resistance work, blowing up railway lines. Even though he wasn't caught red-handed, he was rounded up with his family at machine-gun point and taken into the hills. He lost most of his fingers due to frostbite after being forced to stand in the snow for days and nights on end – and many of his family members didn't survive this ordeal. I used to go to the cinema with them and I taught them a little bit of English. Most of them wanted to return one day to Germany and cause havoc for the people who had destroyed their lives. They kept demanding to be parachuted back into Germany so they could continue their resistance work. Others wanted to immigrate to South America, as far away as they could get from Europe.

It was also during this time that I did a course in driving tanks. We all had to go down to the local quarry and we were taught how to get a tank out of a very big hole. That was an experience I won't forget! It's not every day you get to drive a tank.

Mill Hill, Bury and York   *Jun 1941 – May 1943*

In January 1943 I was granted the rank of staff sergeant. I was proud to have achieved this rank at such a young age. In fact, I still looked like a schoolboy, and I found out afterwards that some of the senior officers had complained and held my promotion up for a few weeks.

But that didn't matter to me. I learnt I was soon going to be leaving England. My chance to travel overseas had finally come!

Chapter 4
Durban and Bombay
Mar – Jun 1943

I was twenty-one years old when I left Greenock, Scotland to travel overseas. I was about to see something of the world and I was full of excitement! I left on a Polish cattle ship, the MS *Sobieski*, that had been converted into a troop ship, and our initial destination was Durban in South Africa.

Unfortunately, the trip to Durban can only be described as nightmarish. With fourteen thousand men on board, the accommodation was cramped and unwelcoming. I was in a room with five other men and we had two sets of three-tier bunks crammed into a tiny space, with only a washbasin between – and to add insult to injury, the basin didn't have any water. Aside from the crew, nearly everyone on the ship became ill. Everyone had been inoculated before the trip and many people, including me, were running a high fever. But worse yet was the food poisoning that we had. I'd lived in the country near a pigsty, and, in my opinion, the food they served us was not fit for human consumption and should have been kept for the pigs. Even the plums, which were usually good, were sour and inedible.

Needless to say, I put myself to bed and tried my best to cope with being extremely ill, but things were soon to get worse. I was travelling with men my own age, but because of my specialist training and high marks, I had been fast-tracked into the position of staff sergeant. A medical officer came down to see me and informed me I was the senior non-commissioned officer on board.

'Get out of bed and get cracking,' he said. 'I need you up and about as acting sergeant major.'

I stared at him from my bunk bed and frowned. 'But I can't,' I said weakly. 'I'm too ill.'

He was an officious type, and he flew into a rage. 'That's an order! Get out of bed!'

'But aren't you going to examine me?' I asked. 'As a medical officer, shouldn't you be finding out about my poor health rather than bullying me?'

At my suggestion he wasn't doing his job properly, he got even angrier. 'I'll have you hung, drawn and quartered!' he yelled. 'Get out of bed!'

I simply looked at him and shrugged. His threat was absurd. 'I'm too ill,' I said firmly, although my heart was pounding wildly by this stage.

He shouted at me some more, but I just closed my eyes until finally he left me in peace. I wasn't going to be bullied by him, and I sensed he knew that. That was the last I saw of him until we reached Durban. The situation on board was so dire that he had to organise ambulances to take hundreds on board to hospital for treatment. I was supposed to be on the last ambulance, but there wasn't enough room. He said he'd organise another, but nothing turned up, so that evening I stayed on board the ship. It was an eerie experience. I was the only one left. There was simply no one else around – no fellow soldiers or sentry or any of the crew. I found myself a nice cabin with a comfortable bed and fell into the best sleep I'd enjoyed since we left Scotland.

In the morning I woke feeling refreshed, and when I wandered to the side of the ship I noticed there were some shops open at the port. I wasn't officially supposed to go off the ship until the ambulance arrived, but as there was no one around I nipped across to the shop and bought some bananas and grapes. I still remember how fresh and wonderful this fruit tasted, and after eating I felt incredibly well, especially after feeling ill for so long.

It was becoming clear that I had been forgotten, so I strolled into town, found a railway station and attached myself to the troops who were travelling. I didn't know any of them, but at least I was with some other soldiers, and I hoped someone would put me in touch with my unit. I ended up almost being forced to board a ship to an unknown destination, although I was clearly in the wrong place and not with my unit. But an officer finally listened to my story and eventually I got a ride to the Clairwood campsite, which was where I was supposed to be.

It was dark and drizzling when I arrived at the campsite with its thousands of army tents. I spoke to one of the officers there and explained the situation, and when everything seemed to be ironed out, I put my gear into my allocated tent at the top of the hill and went in search of some food. Thankfully the canteen was open, so I was able to enjoy a cup of tea and something to eat. Moonlight had come out by the time I returned to my tent, but as I got closer I could see my tent was shaking. Someone was inside! I broke into a run just as a local black man emerged with my kit bag under his arm. I yelled and began to chase him, and he disappeared through a hole in the fence. It was now about eleven o'clock at night. I followed him through the fence, and even though he had a head start on me, I could see his wet footprints on the ground. I could also see he was losing some of my things; they were dropping out of my pack as he ran.

I came across a group of local men who were sitting around a bonfire eating and talking.

'Did you see anyone come this way?' I asked.

'No,' was the defiant reply, even though the footprints went right past them.

Eventually I found my kit bag, and I could see that the thief had tipped all the rest of my gear out on the grass and had disappeared. I collected what I could see in the moonlight and headed back to camp shaking my head. I was thankful I had retrieved most of my things, but in hindsight I realised I had been a bit of an idiot approaching the group of local men. I knew nothing about them, and for all I knew they might have had weapons.

The next morning, I woke with a smile. I was feeling great and looking forward to exploring the local area a little. I was under the impression we wouldn't have much to do but just wait for the next ship to Bombay. But my smile quickly faded when I left my tent and saw my nemesis, the medical officer from the ship.

'You didn't get the ambulance,' he snapped when he saw me.

'It didn't arrive, so I made my own way here.'

'Well, you have to go to hospital,' he said, tapping the clipboard he held. 'You're the only one from the ship not in hospital.'

'But I'm recovered,' I said.

'You can't be. You have to go to hospital and that's an order.'

We argued for some time, but eventually I gave up – he was obviously intent on making my life difficult. It was a strange power game he was playing, but when I arrived at the hospital

I decided it didn't matter. The hospital was neat and clean and had beautiful gardens. I actually ended up enjoying my time there. There were plenty of natural things to keep me interested, including chameleon lizards that changed colour.

Eventually I was released after two lazy weeks, and I had a chance to enjoy some of the surrounding area. I especially enjoyed visiting the Valley of a Thousand Hills, which even then was a popular tourist destination. I enjoyed the spectacular views with literally thousands of hills surrounding the majestic valley created by the Mngeni River, dotted with traditional Zulu homesteads. Not long after this visit, I boarded the SS *Strathaird* bound for Bombay. What a different experience from the first leg of the journey! The SS *Strathaird* was a passenger ocean liner that was now being used as a troop ship. My cabin was comfortable and the food was good – and I really don't remember much more, except that I was wondering how I would ever catch up with my unit, who had already sailed to Bombay some time before.

When I stepped off the ship, Bombay was a sensory overload! It was terribly hot and noisy, and the traffic was mad. The locals didn't appear to use brakes in their vehicles; instead, they used horns. It seemed there were thousands of people crossing here and there and everywhere, and it always seemed a car was just about to crush us. There were also people with handcarts piled with all sorts of things, their carts huge and overloaded, and tricycles that the locals used as taxis. But I didn't have time to get used to the sights and sounds of Bombay and its crazy traffic, because, not soon after arriving, I had a new posting. I was given a piece of paper and railway ticket. My next destination? Allahabad.

Chapter 5
Allahabad
Jul 1943

From Bombay I was posted to Allahabad Fort, where the Ganges and Yamuna rivers meet. Built in AD 1583 by Mughal Emperor Akbar, the fort was an impressive structure with its massive walls and high towers. I remember that it had steps going down from the ground level and when you got to the bottom there was a large banyan tree that looked to be only enormous tree roots. Nearby were a barrel and a padlocked entrance to an underground tunnel. The rumour going around was that a small group of British soldiers had gone to investigate the tunnel and were never seen again. No one wanted to go into the tunnel after that!

I'm not sure why I was posted to Allahabad, as there wasn't really anything for me to do there, and I spent a lot of time just wandering around, looking around the area. There seemed to be some work going on making inexpensive mirrors and manufacturing instruments for operations, but that seemed to be about all.

I noticed straight away that many people who lived there had absolutely nothing, but somehow they survived. Every now and then I came across someone who spoke very good English, dressed in rags. It was quite a surprise. Some of them had been overseas at some point, but had come back and ended up living a life of extreme poverty. It was eye-opening and distressing to see people live like this.

I was only in Allahabad a short time, but I noted that a few British soldiers treated the Indians really badly. I didn't like this at all. There was one British sergeant major in particular who thought he was terribly superior to everyone else. He even organised the seating in the workshop so he was always sitting higher than everyone else. He was also the type of man who didn't take time to get to know the customs of the local people, even something simple like their customs around tea. Most days a man from Afghanistan turned up selling tea. He had a wooden contraption that he carried on his shoulders, with tea leaves and a container of water with a fire underneath it that he could light to boil the water. On one occasion the sergeant major asked the sweeper, who was a newly married young Indian of about eighteen years old, to get him a glass of tea.

The poor young man was obviously poorly educated and quite timid, but he spoke up and said, 'I can't do that,' in Hindu language.

Instead of asking why he refused this request, the sergeant major flew into a rage. 'If you don't do what I tell you to do, I will strap you!'

Still the young Indian man refused to get the glass of tea. 'But I can't do that,' he said over and over, almost like he was pleading.

The sergeant major grabbed up a leather strap and gave him a warning tap. He didn't hit him hard, but the whole situation was utterly unfair. The young man was only a local sweeper and

Allahabad   *Jul 1943*

shouldn't have been put in a situation of fetching things for the sergeant major. I found out later there was some religious reason the young man couldn't bring the tea to the sergeant major – something about not being able to drink tea out of glass – but the story actually got worse when the young man didn't show up at work several days later and I made some enquiries. For Hindus, the cow is sacred, and because he had been hit by a strap made of leather, he was made to pay a fine. But the young man didn't have enough money for the fine – instead, he'd made the tragic error of stealing some money from his father-in-law, presumably because he felt he had no other option, and his father-law reported him to the police. The sweeper was sentenced to six months in prison. I was so angry and upset when I found this out, especially because this awful situation was all due to the ignorance and cultural insensitivity of the sergeant major. It still makes me mad when I think about it. If I had known at the time what was going on, I would have done something to help the young sweeper.

But my time there wasn't all bad. I got to see a lot of local wildlife. I remember seeing a dead donkey that was surrounded by the biggest birds I have ever seen. They were huge, great vultures. They were just like turkeys but two or three times my weight. The other unusual wildlife I saw was some turtles. When the tide went out, they liked to rest on the steep, exposed mud banks, and they were at least a metre in width. I would have looked at them more closely, but as soon as you got near them they slipped off the mud and into the water.

I got invited out now and again by the local people. The first dinner I had was with one of the Indian clerks, and I was amazed to find that his home was utterly beautiful, with marble floors and pillars. He was obviously an important man in Allahabad, although he was doing a poorly paid job for the army.

He and his family were lovely people and very hospitable. They gave me a great big plate heaped with rice, an enormous amount of food compared to what I was used to eating. I had been warned not to refuse anything because it would be considered rude, so I struggled like mad and eventually ate this mountain of rice. But when I had finished, they immediately replaced it with another one! I really didn't want to offend them, so I struggled through another plateful, expecting that to be the end of it. But once again they brought me another plate of rice, as big as the last two!

'I'm very sorry,' I said to them, after staring at the plate for some time, full to the point of bursting. 'I really can't eat all this rice. The first plate was more than I usually eat.'

They looked a little surprised, but took the rice away and replaced it with small sweets covered in edible gold-and silver-wrapping to finish our meal.

It was only the next day that I discovered that even though I had been making lots of enquiries about Indian ways, I still didn't know enough about their customs. There was much hilarity when several of my Indian colleagues explained that I was expected to make a large belching noise when I'd had enough to eat. So I didn't know their rules and they didn't know mine – that I wasn't raised to belch!

I tried my best to record my experiences in my letters to my family, but I pondered that it seemed I had a lot to learn about being posted to India. I welcomed the new challenges.

Chapter 6
Nira
Aug 1943

I received a new posting requiring me to repair equipment, so I travelled by train for three days until I found myself at a place called Nira in India. Of course, travelling by train in India was always chaotic at best. The railway staff were always Anglo-Indian and the thing they liked best in the world was making English soldiers wait. In this particular instance, I went up to the official at the ticket window and he looked me up and down and then simply shut his window and turned his back on me. But I eventually got my seat sorted, so it could have been worse. During my time in India, I saw soldiers who were so frustrated by this rude behaviour that they smashed the windows or broke into the booth via the back door, guns drawn and threatening to shoot the railway official in question if they didn't hand over their tickets. Needless to say, these men got their tickets immediately, but most soldiers with more patience, like me, just suffered the long waits.

As an amusing aside, all the Anglo-Indian men I met spoke English with a Welsh accent. In most cases Welshmen had arrived to work on the railway lines and they had married local girls. Their children, the men I met, would sing with great sincerity songs such as 'The White Cliffs of Dover' and 'I'm Dreaming of a

White Christmas'. As always, India was full of surprises!

Once on the train, there were a new set of challenges to deal with. If you didn't take your seat straight away, someone else would occupy it. In this case, I was travelling on my own, but the train was crowded. People were hanging off the doors and there were even people on the roof. The trains were running for hundreds of miles with people going to different places, so there were always people getting on and off at each stop, and there was a constant battle between people who were already en route and those who were joining. I found my seat and then had the usual task of trying to keep it for the trip.

I had a meal in Poona, which was a major centre that most soldiers went through to get anywhere in India, before going onto Nira. I disembarked from the train at a tiny tin-covered railway station and looked around. It was disconcerting. There wasn't a person in sight and the only creature was a cow with broken legs, hobbling around, which looked like it had been hit by a train. Venturing out from the station, I could see the tracks of hundreds of vehicles. It looked like there had been a large camp with thousands of men there only recently. There was certainly room for hundreds of tents. But for some reason, the camp had been disbanded. I followed the vehicle tracks up the dry, grassy hills – there seemed little point waiting for another train, as the station would only be operational for the duration of the camp.

When I got to the crest, I noticed a Jeep and someone packing up a tent on the next hill. I took off at a brisk pace, probably doing close to a four-minute mile in my eagerness to catch up with them. When I finally got to the hill, sweaty and out of breath, there was a captain and his driver. Unfortunately, the captain was a surly, unpleasant man. He carried on packing up, ordering his driver around, trying to ignore that I was there. It took some time to make him even acknowledge me.

'Will you give me a lift to the nearest army post?' I asked him several times over.

Eventually he deigned to look my way, but what he said next flabbergasted me. 'I can't give you a lift. You could be a spy.'

I was standing in the middle of nowhere in my regulation British staff sergeant's uniform with my heavy kit bag and rifle and he was accusing me of being a spy? It just wasn't credible, but he seemed to have a big grudge about something, and I was bearing the brunt of whatever had happened before I arrived.

'I'm definitely not a spy,' I said to him. 'I've got my papers to prove it.'

The captain's driver seemed a good sort, and he looked very concerned about the situation – but clearly he wasn't in a position to say or do anything. His job was to drive the Jeep and take orders from this man. It was a very tense situation, and I realised as I glanced around the remote location it was also potentially dangerous, because the captain was becoming increasingly angry. He was ready to charge me with being insolent, and, while I watched the veins on his forehead bulge, I became worried that he might actually shoot me. The more he irrationally kept insisting I might be a spy, the more I began to realise that walking fifty miles in monsoon conditions back to Poona, even with my heavy kit, might be the best option after all. Our stand-off came to an abrupt end when the captain and his driver got in the Jeep and drove off, leaving me standing on the hillside looking after them. It was clear that he didn't care if I died of thirst or sunstroke or a snake bite; he just didn't want to be inconvenienced.

Looking around, I thought the best thing I could do was get to the top of the highest hill so I had a better view, and then I could decide what to do next. Up high, I could see for miles, and, in the great distance, there was a Sherman tank and a tank recovery vehicle. Once again I set off, running at speed. I had to get to the tank recovery vehicle before they loaded the tank and drove off – and I noted with some alarm they were making quick work of the job. I was pretty fit in those days, but I was drenched with sweat by the time I caught up with the group of soldiers. There were four of them and they had just finished loading the tank when I arrived. I think they were surprised to see me pop up out of nowhere, but when I told them my story they were friendly and said they would be happy to help me collect my things and give me a lift. After my run-in with the captain, I was highly relieved. I was a higher rank than them, so I could have ordered them to give me a lift, but it was their vehicle and I didn't want to pull rank.

The only catch was that there wasn't any room in the truck cabin, and because I was a stranger they couldn't let me sit inside the tank without risking the wrath of an officer if this was discovered, so the only option left for me was to travel holding onto the tank. Naturally, it started raining soon after we set off, a real downpour. When we finally arrived at Poona several hours later I was soaked through. It was early morning and completely dark. I fell asleep that night on the ground damp and exhausted, wondering where my unit had disappeared to.

In the morning, I got a lift to the Poona Army Headquarters, but the Sikh sentry refused me entry because I didn't have a pass and I didn't know the password. Frustrated, I looked around and spotted a sign that said 'toilet'. The sentry grudgingly gave me permission to use it. To my delight, when I walked into it I quickly discovered that the facility also served the people inside the building. All I had to do was walk through and I was in the headquarters! I guess I deserved a run of good luck after the bad, because the first room I came to was occupied by a general. He was very friendly and listened to my predicament with patience. He was able to inform me that my unit was now situated on Madh Island, which was about twenty-eight miles north of Bombay. His staff arranged for me to have something to eat, and I was soon on a train to my next destination. Who knows what administrative error had caused me to be sent to a disestablished camp in Nira, but I was relieved to be on my way again. I vaguely wondered what Madh Island would be like while I tried to get some sleep on the rickety train ride. I would find out soon enough.

Chapter 7
Madh Island
Aug 1943

I discovered Madh Island was a beautiful but strange place. It was separated from the main land at high tide and appeared to be a cluster of fishing villages and farmlands, although it was clear that, with the army in residence, all the local people had been moved on, because I never saw a civilian. I've been told the island is now a very expensive living area and a resort playground for people who live in Mumbai. When I was there, it was not developed at all, and it was very quiet.

The first thing that struck me was the number of snakes on the island. It appeared that the local people may have worshipped them. There was a temple nearby covered in carvings of cobras and pythons, and the temple had a throne carved out of solid wood that displayed a multitude of snakes, each with the head of a cobra. We had to remove thirty-six snakes to clear our allocated area on the island for two tents that would house six men each. I caught two pythons that were about fifteen feet long doing that job, but I wasn't worried about them because I knew they weren't poisonous. I think because I had caught grass snakes in England, and a mixture of snakes from my time in South Africa, I was naturally interested in the snakes at Madh Island rather than being scared of them. I did treat the cobras with respect, however – they were only about three feet long, but I knew they were highly poisonous. All my army colleagues were nervous of snakes, so I always got the snake-removal job for the army workshop!

There was one snake that we were told we weren't allowed to kill. The locals had been handfeeding this particular python for years before we arrived, and it was as thick as a man's body and about thirty feet long. I think they regarded it as a 'god' snake. The army was building roads that were wide enough for the large army trucks to pass each other. The snake crossed the new road with its head well in the jungle on one side and its tail still in the jungle on the other side. An extraordinary sight!

On the rocks in the distance were Christian graveyards and an old church. The building and graveyard gave the place a slightly spooky atmosphere. I found out later the Portuguese built the Church of St Bonaventure back in the sixteenth century. There was also an old fort, and I was told the locals left dead people up on the towers for the vultures to clean up their remains. I went and had a look and its high towers were filled with soil. Was this story true? I really don't know, but it gave an eerie feel to the place, despite the beauty of its rocky beaches lined with coconut trees.

I did eat well while I was stationed there. I used to go down to the rocks with a wire noose and catch eels that were about the width of my hand. I cooked them up and they were very tasty. And the fresh coconut milk was a wonderful way to finish off a meal – it was cool and refreshing. I used to cut the coconuts down when they were still green, and it was like drinking lemonade without the bubbles.

Madh Island   *Aug 1943*

Another chap and I were given a building made of stone to sleep in. He had one room and I had the other, and each room had two beds. The cover of the beds was made from coconut fibre that had been knotted over a straw mattress, but unfortunately bed bugs had made their home in the knots and straw. You couldn't see the bed bugs in the light of day, but if you switched your torch on at night there were thousands of them. Their bites were awful, leaving large welts that used to itch and irritate – but I was amazed at the brainpower of these small insects. At first I thought they must be climbing up the legs of the bed, so I stood the bed legs in tins of kerosene to prevent this. But then I discovered they weren't crawling up the bed legs at all – they were climbing up the stone walls, walking across the ceiling and dropping onto the mosquito nets that covered the bed, looking for somewhere to get in. I had to admit they were intelligent, but I also had to get rid of them – their bites were driving me to distraction – so I suggested to the chap next door that we float the beds in seawater to kill the blighters. We did one bed at a time for several hours, and that got rid of them. In the hot climate, it didn't take long to dry the beds out.

I would have been very happy to have spent more time at Madh Island, but I was frustrated that once again there wasn't really much I could do, and I really wanted to be useful. The only work that was going on was truck repairs, and my skills were with repairing instruments such as watches, gun sights, binoculars, compasses and the like – they weren't set up for repair work like that. I think the army was going to make Madh Island a base for some combined operations but then changed their mind.

Nevertheless, I was sad to leave this strange island when we got orders to return to Bombay. I got a ride with the sergeant major who was in charge of the truck repairs. He was very good at his job, but he was a completely mad driver. He went flat out going through the villages, his foot to the floor. He seemed to go through spaces that were smaller than the truck, with buildings and shops on all sides, but he never hit anything even though he didn't seem to look where he was going. We ended up lying down because we were afraid to sit up! But we arrived in Bombay before it was dark, and then I travelled the next day to Poona, where I waited to find out where I would be posted next. After the eerie beauty of Madh Island, what should I expect? And when would I get the chance to do something useful for the war effort?

Chapter 8
Ahmednagar
Sep 1943

I was next posted to a small place near Ahmednagar that truly seemed to be in the middle of nowhere. When I got to the railway station, it was late at night and pitch black. With a sinking feeling, I stepped onto the small, empty platform, thinking of my experiences in Nira, but thankfully outside the station was a wiry Indian man with his horse and carriage.

'Where do you want to go?' he asked me in a friendly voice.

'The army workshop,' I said.

He nodded and pointed far into the black distance. 'It's out there. I can take you all the way.'

We agreed on a price and I boarded his small carriage service, expecting to be delivered to the door of the complex. I was surprised when he let me off at the end of a road.

'Are we here already?' I asked, looking around.

'Not far,' he said cheerfully, pointing to a small light in the distant darkness, and, before I had time to think further, he was gone. I shook my head as I walked across the rough ground towards the tiny light, and wondered what the driver had thought 'all the way' really meant.

It was disconcerting walking in the pitch black in a place I had never been to before, but eventually I got to the source of the light, which turned out to be a small building. I found some Indian soldiers and told them I had been posted there. They looked surprised and said there wasn't any room in this place for more people. They conferred amongst themselves and eventually pointed in the darkness towards a tent-shaped shadow.

'We'll have to sort this out in the morning,' said one of them, waving me on. I felt like I had travelled for days just to be told to 'shove off' by his tone, but all I could think of was going to sleep at that point.

When I got inside the tent, I saw there was a coconut-husk bed but nothing else – no lights, no food, certainly no comforts of any kind. Shrugging to myself, I dropped my gear on the ground, crawled onto the bed and fell into an exhausted sleep.

I was woken by growling and snarling. From the fierce sounds, I was immediately worried I might be eaten alive. I couldn't see, but it sounded like there were wild dogs, pigs, leopards and tigers in the tent with me. My heart was racing, but I kept a cool head. I would just have to frighten the hell out of them. I suddenly jumped in the air and yelled as loudly as I could. It worked! The tent was nearly torn to pieces as the creatures fought to escape me. They ran out of the tent as fast as they could go. I got my gun and loaded it, tying a torch to the gun. I could hear snarling and fighting about one hundred yards from where I was. I could see bright green eyes. I fired at the jumping eyes and, abruptly, the fighting ended. I stayed up all night after that – I just couldn't go to sleep – but in the morning there was no sign of any animals, even though I knew I'd killed some. I wondered what other creatures had eaten them.

Ahmednagar *Sep 1943*

It took about a week to get things sorted, but eventually I ended up in a workshop unit on the outskirts of the city. Ahmednagar is a very busy place, but at our base there were our tents and mud buildings and no civilians at all. I soon settled in with a team, teaching them how to repair equipment.

It wasn't long after I arrived that I noticed my socks had big holes in them – which was no wonder considering the amount of walking I had done in this war so far! I went to the store and asked the Indian sergeant sitting at the desk for a pair of socks, noting as I did that the other person in the building was an Indian officer stocking the shelves. It was curious – and even more curious when the sergeant on the front desk ordered the officer to get me my socks.

'How is it you are ordering an officer what to do?' I couldn't help but ask.

'Saab, I am a Pandit Brahmin,' he said.

'And how long have you been in the army?'

'Only three weeks,' he said, smiling at me.

'And you are already a sergeant?'

'That is the least the army could do.'

I processed this information. I knew that 'Pandit' meant a Hindu scholar and Brahmin was the highest, priestly caste in Hindu religion, but it was astounding this man was already a sergeant in the army after only three weeks, and, worse than that, he was ordering an officer around!

As if reading my mind, the sergeant major brought my socks to the desk, avoiding my eye.

I leaned into the desk and spoke slowly to the Pandit Brahmin. 'I think you will have to learn that things are different in the army. I suggest you swap places with the officer back there and he sits at the desk.'

The Pandit Brahmin looked back at me with a lazy expression and handed me my socks. 'I think not, Saab. You do not understand my power.'

I looked at him through narrowed eyes and decided I might make further investigations about this irregular behaviour. His arrogance was grating, his manner smug and condescending.

The next day, when the sergeant major was busy drilling around two hundred men, I went back to the store and discovered the Pandit Brahmin still sitting at the desk. When I brought up the subject of what was appropriate in the army and what wasn't – and that he didn't have the right to order an officer around – things got a little tense.

'Saab, you don't understand my power,' he said smugly, repeating what he'd said the day before.

'Well, you don't understand my power,' I retorted.

'I'll show you how powerful I am,' he said, getting to his feet. 'I will tell the sergeant major to go and fetch my washing.'

'You can't do that!'

'Yes, I can. I am a Pandit Brahmin and he is just a washer caste man, so he has to do my washing.'

'Well, you are going to have to do what I tell you, and if you don't stop this nonsense, I'll have you locked up.' Thinking of a superior officer being treated so disrespectfully by this arrogant person was getting me riled up.

'Saab, I can produce lions, tigers, snakes and crocodiles whenever I want,' he said. 'So don't you threaten me!'

'If you don't produce one of these creatures in the next few minutes, I'm going to lock you up for being insolent.'

We glared at each other while I waited for him to produce one of these creatures, getting madder by the moment. When nothing happened, I tried to move him out the door, but he was a lot heavier than me so I quickly realised that wasn't going to work.

I think he thought I'd given up when I stormed out the door, but I had simply gone for back-up. I approached the first group of soldiers I came to. They were all low-ranking Indian soldiers. I explained that I needed their help in arresting a man, but, to my initial astonishment, they all seemed scared, petrified even, of the Pandit Brahmin and wouldn't help me. It seemed they viewed him as a faith healer and believed him when he said he could conjure up snakes and other creatures. Then I remembered that two of the men in our instrument section were from the same caste. They initially didn't want to help me either – it seemed this man did have some kind of reputation, even amongst other Pandit Brahmins – but we arrested him and placed him in the lock-up. He looked furious and gave me a look of pure hatred.

Later that night I was checking on our workshop, and when I opened the door in the darkness I immediately knew something was wrong. Instinct told me there were snakes in the room, so I shut the door, started up the lighting and went back inside. It didn't take me too long to find two cobras. None of the windows had glass in them, they only had iron bars, so it would have been easy for any snake charmer to have thrown them in there – but it seemed too much of a coincidence that the Pandit Brahmin we had locked up didn't have something to do with this.

Feeling outraged at this possibility, I caught both the snakes and marched over to the lock-up, which was just across from our workshop. I asked the guard to open the door and walked inside. The Pandit Brahmin was sitting on the bottom of three bunks and looked up with an arrogant smile when he saw me.

His expression confirmed my suspicions.

'If you got someone to put snakes in my workshop to poison me, you've made a big mistake,' I said. 'I've caught them and you can have them back.'

I threw the snakes on the floor. They weren't poisonous – a snake charmer must have caught them, and he would have seen to that – but when the Pandit Brahmin saw the snakes his face went pale and he jumped up and got onto the top bunk in a blind panic. He was clearly terrified of snakes. I left him there with them.

The next morning, I had the lock-up opened. As soon as the door was opened, the Pandit Brahmin took off up the road and we never saw him again. I retrieved the snakes and put them in a safe place.

All the other Indian soldiers had thought him a very powerful man, and I found out many of them had gone to him for questionable treatments for their injuries and illnesses as there were no medical doctors or nurses assigned to us there. Most of what he was doing was gobbledegook, and he used to charge people whether or not they felt better afterwards. In fact, he used to sit by the local well, where everyone had to go at some stage, and demand money – and if he didn't get it, he threatened they would get ill! He was actively trying to con people. But it was a curious thing, because word soon got out about what had happened, and from then on I was perceived as being more powerful than him. In effect, I became a faith healer, as people came to see me with their ailments. Of course, I was very upfront that all I could give them was some aspirin, and I refused to take any payment, but I guess with the way some people's minds work, individuals felt better because they had this belief I was powerful. It didn't do any harm, and it even did a lot of good.

Ahmednagar   *Sep 1943*

I guess this Pandit Brahmin never expected to meet anyone who picked up snakes, but providing you pick them up by the backs of their necks, they can't do anything unless they are very big and strong. And most snakes will try to slither away from people, anyway.

It was an interesting time in Ahmednaga. The climate was temperamental, but mainly hot and wet, and that seemed to reflect the ongoing clashes I saw while I was there. There was almost daily conflict between a group of Hindus and Muslims; the situation was not helped when a Hindu sergeant cooked some pork sausages on a Muslim sergeant's stove! In fact, the conflict escalated violently after that stunt into a skirmish where a couple of people got killed and a number of others ended up locked up. It seemed I was partly posted there because I wasn't Muslim or Hindu, so I was a suitable person to help them out at that time.

On a more personal level, many of the soldiers I knew had ongoing problems with underarm sores. The local women used to wash their clothes in the dirty rivers, hitting the clothes with rocks to 'clean' them. I was alarmed when I learnt the people who did our laundry were washing our clothes in the dirty rivers also – although they used to starch them as well. No wonder we were getting sores from our stiff and starched but still unhygienic clothing! The army issued zinc ointment for the sores, but many of the men used this for months without any result. I decided to use some bleach, and I painted that on the sores. It was very painful, but it got rid of them and within a week or two I had new skin.

It was a good experience settling down to doing some repair work with the men there, but the workshop wasn't very well organised, the equipment for repairs was very poor and the work was all a bit unfocussed. I began dreaming about a well-equipped workshop with trained people that could really make a difference to the war effort – but it wasn't until a shopping trip to Bombay that I got a chance to present my idea, which would ultimately change the course of the war for me and send me on adventures I couldn't imagine.

Chapter 9
Poona
Oct 1943

Before I left for Bombay, I asked for permission to meet the most influential general in the army when I was there to discuss my ideas for a workshop to service the Indian and British armies' equipment. I fully expected to be told no, or that I would have to work my way up the army ladder from the bottom rung to make any progress, but to my surprise I was given immediate approval. I presume I was given support from one of the senior officers who knew me and was aware of my particular skills with military technology.

It had been on my mind for some time that there weren't any workshops that were devoted to fixing a lot of equipment that the soldiers relied on. There were teams in place to repair vehicles, but there were no skilled engineers, tools or equipment to repair our men's binoculars, compasses, telescopes, gun sights, rangefinders and other equipment and keep it in working order. The difference between an incorrect gun sight and a correct one was a matter of life and death. A faulty compass could mean getting lost in the jungle. It was crucial that our soldiers had their equipment maintained, and I knew how to design and modify equipment and could also teach.

When I met the general, I raised all of this. I also pointed out that because of the hot and wet jungle conditions, the equipment would need more maintenance than in the cooler climate back home.

'Why are there no workshops?' I asked him.

His reply was to the point. 'Because we can't get the equipment we need in India.'

He looked immediately interested when I offered solutions to this problem. 'I'm good at designing and I can build the equipment we need. I'll make sure we have the best technology to run an efficient workshop. I will be able to build tools and service equipment as good, or even better, than what the army already has back home.'

'But what about skilled people?' he asked. 'I can get you staff, but they won't be trained.'

'I have all the skills you need and I am also a good teacher,' I said.

It was clear he'd been briefed and knew about my background of working for the Sperry Gyroscope Company with what was then state-of-the-art technology and my specialised army training, because he nodded and asked me to go on.

'But I'll need staff who can speak English, because right now I can't speak Indian well,' I said, feeling encouraged by his expression. 'Ideally, I'd like university students who come from families with practical backgrounds, such as jewellers, temple builders, bicycle repairers and the like. I'd like bright young men who can also use their hands. I don't want academics who only know things from books. With a good team, I'm sure I can have an efficient workshop up and running in a short time.'

I took a deep breath. 'Are you interested?'

'Very interested!' he said with enthusiasm.

We talked through the details, and he agreed to provide me with staff and a building in Poona, which was a main army base at that time.

To begin with, I was on my own, and I lived in a tent and had a small, empty, mud-walled room to work in. But soon after, two fine Indian men, Munoswami and Nagarajan, arrived, and they were the first key members of my team. I could tell immediately that they were just the type of men I wanted. Munoswami was a tall man in his thirties of medium to heavy build. I soon discovered he was exceptionally good at repairing binoculars – he could line up the prisms in about two minutes, repairing an astonishing number of binoculars in a day's work. Usually even an experienced man could only manage to repair five or six binoculars in a day. He really had a gift for this, and he was well respected by everyone. I gave him the job of foreman, as he was so reliable. Nagarajan was the youngest and brightest of my team. I gave him the most difficult jobs, such as fixing gun sights, and everything I taught him he picked up with ease. He was very fit, despite his slender, wiry build.

It was a busy time, and there was a great flurry of activity when the general's staff provided me with a big bungalow in Poona, on the main road, opposite the Aga Khan Palace where Mahatma Ghandi was being held under house arrest. The bungalow was built from brick and was large and spacious. It had enough room for a workshop and accommodation for me and my staff. I imagine some rich Indian built it and the army commandeered it. Within a surprisingly short period of time, I had about eighteen staff whom I was responsible for, as well as cooks and drivers who came in to help out but who were housed elsewhere.

When my team was all assembled, I was quietly pleased with this group of men, and as the days became weeks and then months, my first impressions proved to be right. The majority of them were indeed men to be proud of – they were intelligent, enthusiastic and hard-working, but still pleasant people to be around.

All the Indian men had been studying at Madras University before the army asked them to join my workshop unit. I don't know if they were keen to join or not – but we all got on really well, and they were eager students. They respected me and I respected them.

As well as Munoswami and Nagarajan, I had other exceptional Indian men in my team. Gabriel was a tall, courteous Indian man who just got on with whatever I gave him to do. He repaired binoculars and did a very good job. He wasn't adventurous by nature, but he was happy to venture out with me when the time came for us to move from Poona. Lurdu Swami was also one of my right-hand men – he was a Pandit Brahmin, but nothing at all like the Pandit Brahmin I'd met in Ahmednagar! He was tall and hard-working but he had a laid-back attitude to life. Kesavan was also a valued member of my team, a good-looking younger man with glossy thick hair that he liked to keep immaculate who also applied the same level of care to his work. Dhanaphal was also quite young, but was a very good binocular repairer. Mohamed Ali was the only Muslim in the group, but he was the most pleasant of men and there were never any problems between him and the others. He was a machinist so spent his time making parts.

Of course, not everyone was exactly what I had hoped for. Rajan was with us for only a short period, and it was soon clear that his father must have pulled some strings for him to join my workshop. He was a pleasant enough chap, but he wasn't very bright and really didn't have a clue even after being repeatedly shown things. He must have decided repair work wasn't for him, because he just disappeared one day and we never saw him again. The only other Indian in my team I had any problem with was Singh, my storeman. He was a very lazy individual and was always complaining about his boils, that he couldn't sit down in the storeroom but nor could he stand up. And he complained for some time that his wife wasn't getting her money, although we were faithfully sending it on a regular basis. It turns out the real problem was we weren't sending money to his second wife! It was even more complicated when I found out the two wives didn't know about each other.

I also had some European men in my team. Bill was a non-technical guy who turned out to have a natural gift for organisation. I used him for all my administration and liaison. He came from London and was ever so well liked by everyone – he was a very popular man who was good at getting things done. We ended up being great friends, and he was the sort of bloke who would talk to everyone and anyone.

By contrast, one of my men who repaired compasses, Charlie, turned out to be a real rogue. Back in England, he had been part of a gang of fur thieves (back in the day when women still wore furs). We used to have our food parachuted in, and I discovered after a while that he was stealing food from one of the drop points, taking the best fruit and other goods for himself. I confronted him. I gave him the choice of adding sentry duty to his usual duties or else I would report him. He was a weak man and immediately took the sentry option – and after that he didn't have time to go out stealing food! Problem solved.

Ted was a very good mechanic. In civilian life he had been a jewellery shop assistant. I had to wonder how good he had been at his job, however, as he was constantly buying glass jewels instead of the real thing. The glass jewels were rather obvious as they all had marking moulds, whereas the real Burmese jewels were in queer shapes and by the colour you could tell they were authentic. I used to tell him he was only buying glass, but he wouldn't listen to what I had to say! But he was a great guy and we got on well.

A couple of my European men had a fondness for the ladies. Dick, who used to repair gun sights, often had a lady friend in his sights too – but I'm not sure how successful he was with them. Frank, by contrast, was very good-looking, and he was always finding a woman to get into bed with – but he only worked with me for a very short period, as he ended up totally diseased. He contracted leprosy, which was very common in that region, and I suspect he had syphilis and other diseases as well. I don't know what became of him in the end, but it would seem his womanising was his downfall.

Once my team was assembled, we had a mountain of work to get through. Our first task was to build the equipment we needed to do the repair work, and then we would tackle all the repairs. There were twenty-six thousand men in the 36th Division, and they all had equipment that we needed to maintain for them! It was a big job, a huge responsibility, but I was confident my team was up for the challenge.

I had already drawn up designs for the test equipment that I wanted made, and I had begun sourcing materials we could use. From old junk shops, I sourced old optical instruments that could be adapted. I used a piece of the Bombay tram rail as a base for a collimator, which is a device for aligning the prisms in binoculars. I saw immediately that tram rail was easy to source, and very heavy and strong. It seemed everywhere I looked there was material that we could use to build the equipment we needed – I just had to think outside the square!

My team was exceptionally clever and they took instruction very well. In no time, they had taken my designs and instructions and made the equipment we needed, and then they started the work of repairing soldiers' gear. I was especially concerned with making sure men's binoculars were up to scratch, because they were used at relatively short distances to observe the Japanese. This was a special challenge because, in jungle conditions, they were soon full of fungus, so we needed to maintain a terrific turnover to keep them clean and operational for our troops.

This is an aside, but in general the Japanese equipment I saw was far superior to our own. The binoculars were no exception – the Japanese ones I saw were a beautiful German design, whereas ours were very clunky and similar to what was used in World War One. But thankfully in this instance the metal the Japanese binoculars was made from disintegrated in the jungle environment, so ironically our old-fashioned technology ended up being better!

My workshop was soon running efficiently. Headquarters organised to send all the binoculars, compasses, gun sights and other equipment to us when units were on leave so we could do all the work during their rest period. Trucks would bring the equipment in to us – thousands of pieces of equipment at a time – and then return to take them away. We had to work hard to keep up with the demand, but it was satisfying. The men worked twelve-hour shifts and I worked nine hours of each shift myself. That meant I only got six hours' sleep a night, but I was happy to be finally doing something useful for the war effort. The Indian men, in particular, were happy to do long hours, as they felt they had a special job. They also knew I was working even harder and I would to do anything for them.

It was a wonderful time, and the fact that my Indian men were enthusiastic students made it even better. It was a happy atmosphere, and I got on well with just about everyone who was involved. I also started to pick up the local market Indian language, and when I went back to India years later all the taxi drivers could understand me.

It was a lot of hard work though, with little time to do anything else except sleep and eat. I used to say to the cooks to not make English food as they made such a rotten job of it, so we existed pretty much on a diet of rice and curry. I noted that very few Indians had dysentery, while the English soldiers seemed to suffer from it constantly, so I thought eating the local diet was a good idea.

General Francis Festing visited the workshop on occasion, and I was very impressed by the man. He was a very pleasant person to talk to, and it wasn't long before I had a good relationship with him. He used to wear three watches so he could be sure that the time was accurate. I made it one of my jobs to maintain his watches for him. He also smoked a curved pipe but had a habit of biting through the base, so I used to repair his pipes also. I found he was a good man for discussing things on an equal level. We became quite close with time, and, even though he didn't have any technical knowledge, he listened very carefully to my ideas. He struck me as a person with a natural talent for leadership, and he was also very level-headed.

It was a busy and rewarding time, although I was well aware that not every soldier was happy. In general, the morale of the soldiers was very low because of the defeats we had been suffering in Burma. I know of at least two officers who committed suicide near Poona, and the rates of mental illness was very high. There was a mental hospital called Doolally, a severe-looking place with twenty-foot high walls close to road and rail, and that is where the saying 'going doolally', as in 'going mad', comes from. A lot of people used to go to India and sign on for eight years, and they just couldn't take it and ended up incarcerated in this facility.

There was another incident that reflected the strangeness of some people's minds at this time. There was a captain in the same building as me who one day ordered his servant to bring his daughter to his room. It wasn't long before we heard gunfire. When we ran to investigate, we found the terrified daughter standing against the door while her father fired bullets around her. It was a terrible situation! We disarmed the man, and although he was of superior rank and I wasn't supposed to report him, I did just that.

But work remained my primary focus, especially when I was told there was a plan for our side to capture a Japanese-occupied airfield in Arakan. The workshop's next challenge was to waterproof the equipment of the lead beach assault team of the 36th Division in preparation for this offensive. I also had plans for modifying two three-tonne trucks that I had been given to turn them into mobile workshops, so that if we were posted to Arakan and Burma, we would still be able to repair instruments. I fell asleep between my shifts exhausted but excited by the challenges of what we were doing and what might happen next.

Chapter 10
Nashik
Nov 1943

I was in the midst of waterproofing equipment when I was ordered to Nashik, and I had instructions to wait there until needed. I wasn't sure what I was supposed to be doing, but I left Munoswami in charge of the workshop, confident I could leave my men to continue the work as efficiently and precisely as before. I boarded a train.

There wasn't much to see at Nashik. It was a dry, sandy place with a few clear-water rivers, and the only building of significance was an Indian temple on a hill, way up above the hot plains. I was ordered to stay in a small storeroom that was pretty much in the middle of nowhere. It had no doors and it was fenced by cactus plants. There was very little for me to do while I was there, so I spent my time studying the local wildlife – there were snakes, scorpions, lizards and all sorts of other interesting creatures to contemplate.

In particular, the place seemed to be full of lizards that looked prehistoric. They were less than a metre in length, but very ugly-looking. They had expanding fans on their necks, so when they quarrelled they blew up bright blue and orange fans, although the rest of their bodies were dull. They used to dive into the water and stay underneath for about twenty minutes. They were quite fascinating to look at – and some of the snakes were different from anything I had seen before as well.

I was only there for a matter of weeks, but it was a very lonely time and I missed my men and the rhythm of work in my workshop. To get something to eat, I had to walk a couple of miles across the sandy desert to an army store nearer Nashik. I had a number of conversations with the corporal who ran the store, and he turned out to be an interesting character. He had been in the cavalry, riding horses, which was a passion for him – but as time went on, the horse riding became too much. He was put in charge of the store, but it wasn't something he enjoyed.

'But you've done your eight years,' I said. 'Why don't you go home to England?'

The answer was compelling. In the eight years, he had constructed a whole new life. He had a wife and family, with plenty of money and security.

'There is no point going back to England,' he said. 'I'm better off here.'

'So what don't you like about your role?' I asked.

He pointed to the coding on the paperwork on his desk. 'I don't have a clue what any of this means.' He picked up a form. 'If somebody wants an X232, I don't know how to help them. I don't even know if I have any in stock!'

I immediately saw an opportunity to make myself useful, and his look of relief when I offered to match the equipment with the codes was worth all the work it entailed. I methodically went through his storeroom, so, when I had finished, he knew exactly what he had and what each of the codes meant.

Nashik   Nov 1943

He wanted to repay me for my efforts. I noticed he had a small anvil on his desk, which is a primary tool for metal workers, and I thought some of these would be useful for the workshop, so I asked if he could send me eight for when I got back. It seems he was still confused about items under his charge, though. In due course, the anvils arrived, but instead of eight anvils that were the size of a hand each, each of them weighed half a tonne! It would seem he didn't know they made anvils for instrument work – he ordered me the size that blacksmiths use!

So I spent my days studying the creatures that lived in Nashik and helping the corporal in his storeroom. Then, not long before I was ordered back to Poona, like a mirage, columns of soldiers appeared in the distance, walking alongside the railway line. They were men back from fighting in Burma, and when they got closer, I saw they were in a dreadful state. They didn't have any proper clothing – their uniforms were rags, and some were only wearing their underclothes – and they didn't have any weapons because they had thrown away their rifles when they ran out of ammunition. They were horribly thin and nearly all of them were suffering from malaria and dysentery. It was a terrible sight to see these men, defeated and severely depressed. They had lost so many men, their friends killed by the Japanese or by illness in the unforgiving jungle. They were also mutinous – they had lost all their officers, and they blamed the officers for running away and leaving them, when the truth was that the Japanese had likely shot them. If there weren't enough bullets to shoot everyone, the Japanese were always good at targeting the officers. But the soldiers didn't want to believe that.

There was a young chap who had been made a lieutenant but was clearly out of his depth. He was panicking and the soldiers weren't paying any attention to him, except for some of them who looked at him with murderous intent in their eyes. I spoke to him and offered to help as I had plenty of army experience, but he decided he'd try to handle the men himself. There was little I could do after he had refused my offer.

Back in Poona, I wondered how he had fared in such mutinous conditions, but I had a situation of my own with one of my men to deal with. Nagarajan had been temporarily posted to another workshop for a short time, and the captain there had decided to demote him. I was furious when Nagarajan rejoined our workshop and I discovered what had happened. I had a blazing row with this particular captain. Here was my best instrument repair technician, a highly skilled man with a bright future, who had been demoted by an idiot of a captain simply because the captain wanted to promote one of his vehicle mechanics and had to tally up the numbers! It made no sense, and Nagarajan had done nothing wrong, nothing at all to deserve a demotion – if anything, he deserved a promotion! Thankfully, I had the general's ear on this matter and soon had the situation sorted.

It was after I had sorted this personnel issue that I again considered what I had witnessed in Nashik with those columns of dispirited men. Things clearly weren't going well for our side in Burma and Arakan, and the word was a new campaign would be launched in the New Year – and this time some of my team and I would be involved. I wondered how we would fare.

Chapter 11
Bawli Bazaar
Feb 1944

With new orders, some of us took a train to Calcutta while the rest of my team drove there to set up a new workshop base. When I was satisfied the workshop was working smoothly, I left my team in Calcutta under the leadership of Bill and Munoswami and I travelled across by sea to Cox's Bazaar. From there I travelled south over very bad roads to Bawil Bazaar. The roads were unsealed clay tracks that in monsoon conditions would have become swamps, but when I travelled on them the roads had dried out and there were big potholes everywhere. Every time the driver hit a pothole, I hit my head on the machine gun stashed above me. It was most unpleasant.

I had mixed feelings about being in Arakan, away from my team. The Akyab Airfield beach assault had been partly a success but mostly a failure, in my view. Several men drowned during the landing. The water was much deeper than the army had thought, and with their heavy gear, rifles and ammunition, many of these men didn't have a chance. It was such a waste of young men's lives. In addition, the 7th Division ended up being surrounded by the Japanese and had to escape on foot, leaving behind valuable equipment. I was there to repair any instruments that were needed urgently, with everything else going to my team.

The army set up base at a place called Bawli Bazaar, a small village that the 36th Division had taken over. This part of Arakan was hot and terribly dry. It was rugged landscape, a mixture of hills, rocks and sea – the area now awash with our troops – and it was chaotic, to say the least. We made ourselves comfortable in the shops of a village square, all the buildings made of bamboo. It seemed to me a lot of people were treating the experience as though it were a summer holiday camp, and not many seemed concerned that Japanese might be about, even with all the fighting of late. I thought it was prudent to take action, so boiled my clothes and sheets in dirty leaves so they were camouflaged.

It wasn't long after I arrived that the word came that the army were looking for volunteers to go to the site of the recent fighting and bring back as many spare parts as they could from the blown-up vehicles. I didn't hesitate in volunteering. I was there to help the war effort in whatever way I could, even if it might be dangerous. I believed common sense would probably keep me safe, so I wasn't nervous. I set off with a group of about fifteen men.

Our team was a mixed group of diverse individuals. A Canadian major was in charge. We called him 'O.C.', short for 'Officer Commanding'. He was an older man and a level-headed, reasonable sort. Taffy was also one of the team. He was a Welshman who had run into trouble with his own unit – he'd served a number of weeks in an army prison for his bad behaviour – and he had been transferred to help us with odd workshop tasks. He was a skinny fellow and I could tell he and trouble were never too far apart. I would only find out more about his personality later on.

Another of our group was nicknamed 'Bunny', and I don't know now what his real name was. I have no idea why he volunteered for this mission, as he was as twitchy as a rabbit. Perhaps he'd been encouraged as he was a good motor mechanic, but he was an extremely nervous individual, totally unsuited for wartime exploits. By contrast, Tommy was a part of this unit and he was pretty tough. He was a short, wiry individual, a Glasgow Gorbal, and he knew how to fight with cut-throat razors. He had a Kukri, which was a curved knife that the Gurkhas famously used. It was a lethal weapon, and he practiced by throwing his knife at a tree, thinking of the tree as the enemy. He used to throw the Kukri by the tip of the blade and it spun a bit like a boomerang. He had deadly aim. Needless to say, he wasn't a person to cross.

The group of us set off carrying spanners and other tools to remove spark plugs, carburettors and anything that might be salvageable and useful from the vehicles, as well as our weapons and gear. All was going well until an individual, halfway up the jungle-covered hill, starting shooting at us – but fortunately he wasn't a good shot. We had found an old tin bath that was useful for putting spare parts into – now the bath served for providing us with some extra cover as well.

In my experience, I didn't find the Japanese to be very good shots. I don't know if this was because they didn't have the right training or if there was something wrong with their guns. I found a couple of their rifles at one stage and couldn't hit anything with them, and I didn't know how to adjust the sights as they were metric, whereas ours were imperial. Their design was completely different from our guns, also.

One of the men found a primus stove during our salvage mission. They were quite common at the time and good for cooking. It burned kerosene and produced a nice blue flame. In due course, we got back to Bawli Bazaar, and we were settling back into our occupied shops when I noticed one of the men pouring petrol into the stove.

'Anyone got some matches?' he asked.

Another soldier handed him a box.

'Don't light it!' I shouted from across the room, but I was too late.

Before I could stop him he lit the stove. There was a loud explosion as the stove ignited into a huge fireball and the bamboo building began burning. Within minutes, the entire square was ablaze. We had no means to put out the fire, so it was chaos as everyone ran, taking as much of their gear as they could. I had a portable unit I was using for repairs. It was on folding legs, but when I grabbed it to throw it onto the street, the legs snapped. Thankfully no one was injured, but our base camp had now burnt to the ground. The orders quickly came to move camp, this time inland, into the jungle.

Needless to say, the mood was very sombre.

Chapter 12
Buthidaung
Feb 1944

The next day I set up my workspace in a well-protected and concealed spot in the jungle, between two large boulders on a dried-up river bed. This area of Buthidaung in Arakan was bushier than Bawli Bazaar had been. I deliberately chose a spot beyond the camp perimeter so I could get on with the urgent work that I had to do and I could avoid the constant enquiries from individuals who wanted me to look at their watches or binoculars. My portable workbench was surrounded by jungle and was very effectively camouflaged. We usually slept in pairs, so later in the day Bunny and I built two slit trenches, each the size of small bed and up to our chins. One I left open-topped and in an obvious place, but if Japanese decided to throw grenades into it I knew we would be sleeping in the other slit trench, our twelve-inch-high mosquito net camouflaged by leaves. Bunny was less nervous knowing he would be with me for the night and that I had a strategy for sleeping out in the jungle that involved identifying every night-time noise before turning in.

Much later, when the sun was beginning to set, nine young men appeared near our campsite. I went out to say hello. It turned out they were machine gunners from Manchester. They had been walking all day and were dirty and exhausted.

'Do you mind if we set up camp near you?' asked one of them.

'Not at all, but I suggest you camouflage your slit trenches and mosquito nets,' I said.

'Camouflage?'

'It's easy. All you need to do is put leaves over your mosquito nets and then you'll be really hard to see.'

'There are no reports of Japanese activity in the area,' said another of the men, pulling out his shovel and yawning as he did so.

'Even so, you can never be too careful out here,' I said.

They set to work, and when I looked later I saw they had dug their trenches in straight military lines, all lined up in a neat, tidy row. I shook my head. I know they had been taught that in the army, but in jungle conditions you had to be more cunning. It seemed they had been too exhausted to take my advice. I was about the only person in camp who had gone to the measure of camouflaging my sleeping area, but a sixth sense told me I needed to be careful, even if the official reports were that the area was clear of Japanese.

Unfortunately, my sixth sense proved to be accurate, and that night a terrible tragedy occurred. The Japanese crawled quietly down the riverbed and spotted my comrades' mosquito nets erected along the upper edge of the water. Nine Japanese silently approached the sleeping men, and one stood at the foot of each of the nine trenches. When the signal came, they bayoneted each of the men. The Manchester gunners never had a chance.

I was woken by yelling, and as soon as I realised what was happening I quietly prepared my Sten gun and put on my boots.

Despite the heat, Bunny was also wearing his jungle uniform, but he hadn't moved and it was clear he was waiting for orders.

'Prepare your rifle,' I whispered. 'I'll need you to cover me. Follow when it looks safe.'

Looking as scared as I felt, Bunny nodded and quietly loaded his rifle. When he was ready I told him I needed him to cover me while I made for our other slit trench. The moon was covered by clouds, so it was difficult to see. I managed to slither over the loose stones of the riverbed, but one of our men, a gunner guarding the back of the camp, opened fire on me. I flattened myself behind one of the boulders and listened for a moment. It was clear the gunner couldn't bring his line of sight low enough and he was hitting the riverbank. When my breathing had evened, I slowly and quietly slithered out of range, wishing I wore the Japanese rubber jungle boots instead of the British Army hobnail ones. Each step seemed to make an enormous amount of noise.

I discovered a lance corporal still asleep in the back of a truck. I woke him and he immediately pushed aside his green jungle net and stood up, dressed only in his underwear. Unlike the rest of us, who were sunburnt and quite dark, he was white and shone like a beacon in the moonlight that had just appeared from behind clouds. Despite the sporadic firing taking place, it seemed to take him ages to understand the Japanese were attacking our camp.

Finally, everything registered, and he fell to the ground and then spent several awkward moments trying to put on his jungle uniform. It would have been humorous under other circumstances, but there wasn't anything funny about our situation – I realised we were now in for the fight of our lives. Meanwhile, the sounds of firing were increasing and all around us grenades were going off, setting several vehicles alight. Savage yells and the crackle of machine and Tommy guns filled the air.

'Who goes there?' shouted some of my comrades in the traditional manner. Most received a bullet or grenade in reply.

Bunny caught up with us just as the lance corporal had finished putting on his uniform.

'What should we do now?' Bunny asked. He looked terrified.

'You need to find cover,' I said. 'I'm going to the main camp, to the slit trenches there.'

The lance corporal and Bunny dived into a nearby rubbish trench and I set off, keeping low to the ground, finally reaching the main slit trench area. It was hard to tell who was friend or foe in the dark conditions, so it was with relief I heard the voice of a chap we referred to as 'The Bomber'. He was from the artillery section and had owned a garage in civilian life. He had a very distinctive English voice and had visited my portable workshop from time to time to see what I was up to.

'It's me,' I called out and slithered into the trench beside him.

'It's good to see you, Hennessy,' he said in his familiar voice. 'But I think it would be best if you try to get to the next trench. Taffy's there on his own.'

It was clear that I couldn't stay where I was. Six men were now crushed into a space designed for three.

'I'll be off then,' I said. 'Can you give me cover?'

The Bomber nodded, and when they opened fire, I ran across to the next trench and dropped down, my heart pounding. I looked across at Taffy. He seemed to be in some kind of trance, and he was muttering loudly to himself.

'Shut up!' I hissed.

He continued muttering words that made no sense.

I shook him, looking at him closely. His eyes were glassy and his expression was quite demented.

'Shut up!' I said again.

He finally fell silent.

It was then I became aware of the intense pressure on my bladder. Bursting to urinate, I decided that Japs or no Japs, I had to do something about it. I knew if I peed on the dried leaves it would make such a noise the Japanese would hear. So I peed on the wall of the trench, but all the soil started to crumble and fall down onto the very dried leaves I had been trying to avoid. It was creating a heck of a noise, but at that point I just had to keep going.

'Shut up!' Taffy started shouting at the top of his voice. 'Shut up!'

'Shhh!'

Just as I had finished, we both heard the sound of marching. To my horror, Taffy jumped up and started shouting at the top of his lungs, 'Hooray! It's the Welsh! They're coming to save us!'

'Shut up, you fool!' I hissed, trying to pull him down. 'It's the Japanese.'

He kept shouting.

'It can't be the Welsh,' I hissed. 'They're too far away.'

He finally went quiet and then we both stared into the dark. I fully expected a grenade or bayonet at any moment and cursed the fact I was sharing a trench with someone so unstable.

Suddenly there was the noise of more gunfire and from the direction of the burning vehicles came the sound of a Jeep being started without success. There was silence and then the sound of the Jeep starting again, this time with success. I could just make it out, moving from the centre of the camp, and then it crashed its way along the track, down into the riverbed, up the other bank and then round the bend out of sight.

There was a sudden heavy burst of firing and the noise of grenades from the direction of the officers' mess. We found out later that the Japanese had seen the sign to the officers' mess but, unbeknown to them, they had walked into a trip. A quick-thinking corporal with a few infantry soldiers was in two facing slit trenches and they waited until the Japanese were walking past before opening fire. The Japanese managed to throw one grenade and it landed in one of the slit trenches, cutting the wristwatch of a radio technician. But he had the presence of mind to pick up the grenade and throw it back. None of our men were injured.

Things were becoming much quieter when I realised that someone was escaping along the riverbank. It was too dark to see if he was friend or foe, so I left the now eerily quiet Taffy behind in the slit trench and began following him. Because my boots were making so much noise, I ended up following him on my knees, which was very painful. But he appeared to be wounded – he was moving very slowly, so I was making progress. Just when I felt I was gaining ground, he slipped up the bank and into the undergrowth, however. I followed him up the bank at a different place. It was only when it was finally daylight that I found him, dead and lying flat on his back. He was Japanese. He looked young and I suddenly felt sorry for him and his family, and all of us in this sorry mess.

I started to make my way back to camp, but it was slow progress, as I'd torn up my knees. Eventually I came across a bamboo building as the sun was beginning to go down. It was on stilts with stairs going up to the main building, presumably to keep the snakes out. I found a couple of our men already camping there, so I joined them, all of us too tired to share more than a few words.

That night the building creaked and groaned around us,

Buthidaung *Feb 1944*

the bamboo making a terrible noise in the wind. But suddenly there was a more ominous noise – there was the distinct sound of someone climbing the stairs. Could it be the Japanese? I was instantly awake, noticing my companions were alert also.

We looked at each other and silently held our Sten guns at the ready, but the noise faded away and then there was just the sound of the building creaking. In the morning we crept down the stairs and discovered a dead Japanese man. Next to his body was a tin filled with peas and beans, and some leftover opium pills. I only hope the opium pills gave him some relief while he was dying.

I got back to base camp that day and the place was in turmoil. In all there had been probably 150 Japanese men in the attack, just as many on our side and an even number of dead on both sides. Our side was now blasting the surrounding hillside with all the guns we had.

I soon had a new assignment. It seemed our long-range guns weren't working, and the general wanted me to go and see what was wrong and to fix what I could. A driver took me close to the site, which was about eight miles from our base camp, and I climbed the rest of the way on my own. It was a sorry sight because all the guns had been sabotaged, but it looked like there were parts I could salvage. The gunners were mortified by the situation. It seems the sentries had been duped by a group of Japanese wearing Indian uniforms and had let them in, not realising they were the enemy until after they had gone. They had smashed up our guns. In the sentries' defence, the Japanese had driven up in captured British vehicles and spoke Hindi, and none of the men there had seen either Indian or Japanese close-up before, so the deception would have been easy, but nonetheless they were in bad spirits.

I was just about to head back to my driver when Japanese mortar came raining down. The explosions were huge and utterly terrifying. I dived for a slit trench that was only about twelve inches deep so I had to lie in it. I couldn't tell where the shells were coming from and I just had to wait helplessly while the earth shook and rattled around us. I found out later the Japanese had taken over one of the railway tunnels and were firing from there. The attack seemed to last forever, but eventually mortar fire ceased and I gingerly climbed out of my trench, a gunner nearby doing the same.

'Glad that's over,' said my companion, running a shaky hand through his dirty hair.

'Me too,' I said, not voicing my unsaid fear that the shelling might start up at any moment.

I went to check on the guns again, but now discovered they were completely unsalvageable after the mortar attacks. They had been blown to smithereens. I considered my course of action and decided I was best to head down the hill and hopefully catch up with my driver and get out of there. At the very least, I would probably be safer near the bridge the army was building in the area. I set off at a brisk pace, but my heart was in my mouth when I discovered blown-up pieces of a truck farther down the hill. Had the driver survived? At that point, more mortar fire sounded, so I took cover for the next twenty minutes, waiting for the shells to cease, all the time wondering about the fate of my driver. When the mortar fire finally ended, I took the opportunity to examine more pieces of the truck, and then it suddenly dawned on me that what I was looking at was a different model. I almost laughed out loud when I realised the absurdity of the situation.

But that still didn't solve my problem of getting back to base, so

I started the long trek, walking in the dry drains by the side of the road that in monsoon weather would be overflowing with water. I had only gone a mile or so when I saw a cloud of dust coming up behind me. It could only be one thing – one of our trucks. I was in full uniform, so when the truck came closer I waved it to stop. It didn't stop – but it slowed down enough so that I could scramble on the back. I quickly realised it was my truck, and my Indian driver, who had previously been quite black, was now very white. He didn't want to stop, and mortar fire was starting up again. We had a shouted conversation, and it turned out he had been sitting in the truck, waiting for me, when the truck next to him was blown to pieces. Part of a shell had come through his truck and through my seat and then out the windscreen. It was no wonder he didn't want to stop. He drove like a demon until we were back at base camp.

Much later, when the shelling had finally stopped and the attack was over, it turned out many of our men were missing, including the lance corporal and Bunny. They got lost in all the confusion and it took them several days to find their way back to our lines. They only found their way out by hearing our army trucks. Both were in a severe state of shock and suffering from exposure. Bunny, in particular, became seriously ill from stress.

The hero of the day was a noisy, egoistical workshop store man who had constantly boasted about what he would do to the 'little yellow bastards'. He was the man whom we'd heard in the Jeep, but unfortunately the Japanese got hold of him. He was a huge, strong man and fought back valiantly, but he received seventeen bayonet wounds and was left for dead. It was something of a miracle, but he recovered, and, from the regular bulletins we received, we later learnt that he returned invalided to his wife in South Africa.

The other hero of the day was the cook assigned to the machine gunners who had been so brutally murdered. In the commotion, his truck was set on fire and he went completely berserk. It turned out his truck was full of food that he had stolen and hoarded for a birthday celebration for one of the chaps who had died. Anyway, he was so riled he ran straight into the Japanese with his machine gun and ended up killing fifteen of them. He got an award for his bravery.

Words can't fully describe how I feel about this Japanese attack, but it made me realise that the old cliché 'war is hell' unfortunately is very true. I am just thankful that I survived, as did the men I knew personally, but I still think of the men who died, especially the nine young men from Manchester, and the grief at such loss of life still feels raw.

Military College of Science

Shopping in India

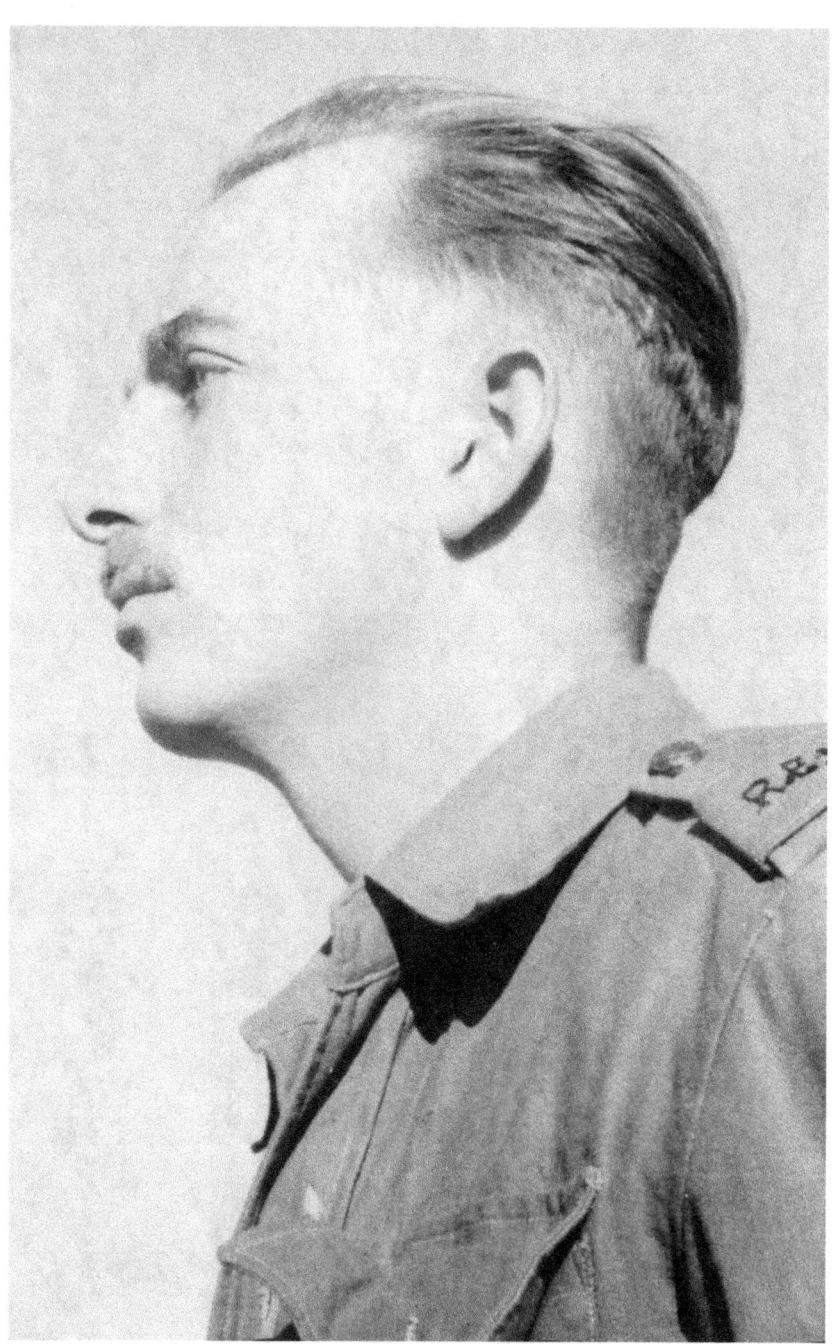
Brian Hennessy while in India

Bombay swimming pool

Children in India

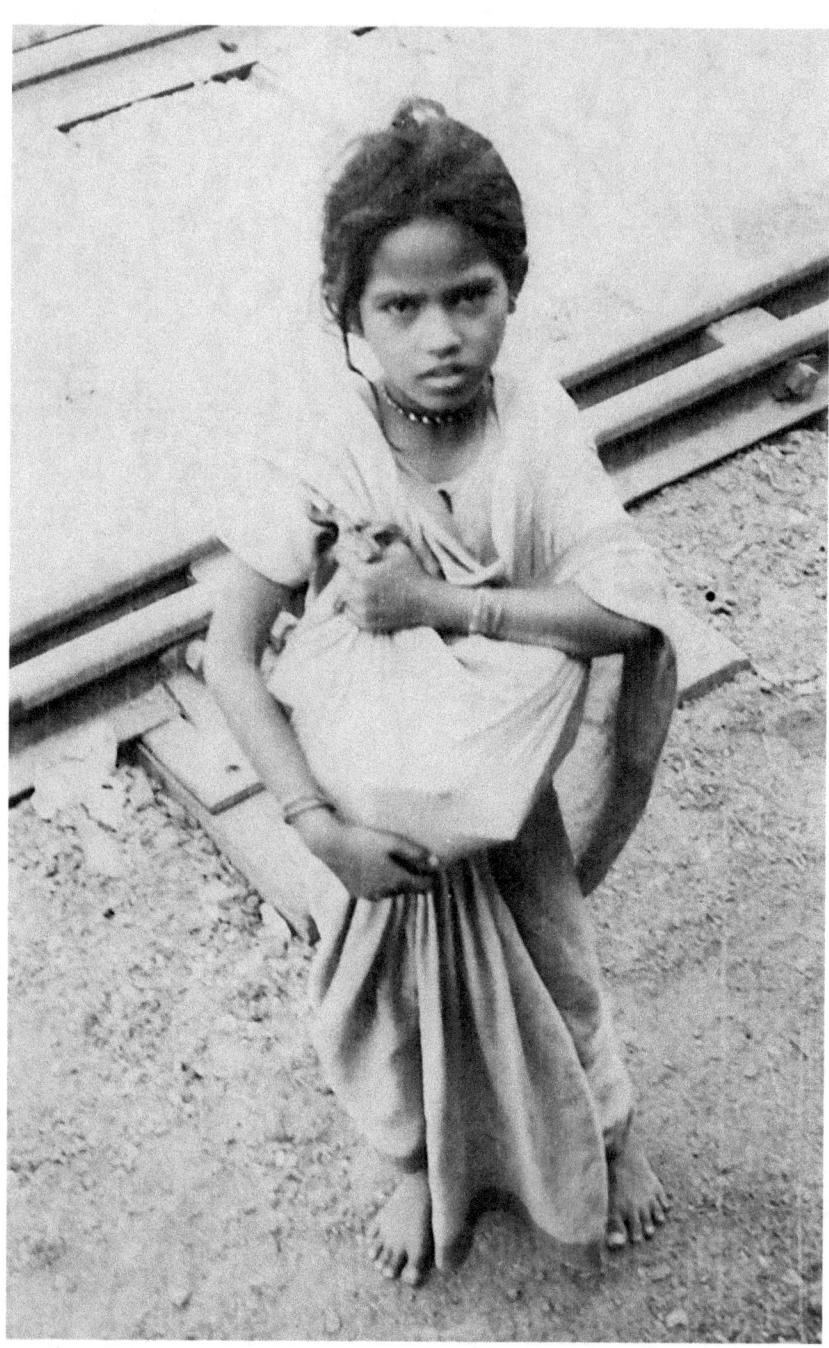
Girl begging by the railway in India

Above: Local family in India

Left: Brian Hennessy in India

The view from the Temple in Nashik, India

Rural scene in India

One of the many temples Brian Hennessy visited, location unknown

Above: Brian Hennessy – photo taken by brother Lionel in a restaurant in Poona

Right: Christmas celebration in Nashik, India

Chambu Lama Temple

Parade before leaving India

Another temple, location unknown

In the jungle in Arakan

Travelling workshop used in Burma

Brian Hennessy after being in Burma and being severely ill

Kazue and Rose, friends of Brian Hennessy in Japan

Chapter 13
Buthidaung
Mar 1944

A month after the Japanese attacked Buthidaung I was still vigilant about other possible attacks, but I was busier than ever repairing instruments for the 36th Division, with my team back in Calcutta also hard at work. There wasn't much respite from work apart from eating and sleeping.

We used to get our food in large tins that were four feet high. The food was parachuted in and each tin would have enough food for eight men for a day – or eight meals for one man. Unfortunately, insects usually ate the raisins and biscuits before we got to them, but the tinned stuff was okay. We ate a lot of Spam and South American bully beef. For a while there, I was eating bully beef three times a day. I quite liked it, although I was quickly getting tired of eating the same thing all the time.

I often used to think the Japanese could easily find any of the Allied camps for two reasons. Firstly, it was easy to track the British Army by the discarded bully beef cans. Secondly, most of the British and American soldiers smoked. The smell of cigarettes easily let anyone know where the different camps were. I realised we could hardly stop soldiers from smoking, but I was always aware of how easy we were making it for the Japanese to find us. It was even more obvious when men smoked at night because you could see the glow of the cigarette ends.

I spent a lot of time during this period fixing gun sights, and I was concerned that many of our larger guns, like a twenty-five-pounder, fired shells in a trajectory, that is, a shell that goes up in the air in an arc. To my mind, that didn't seem very suitable for jungle conditions when fighting the Japanese. I was interested in guns that fired straight, like rifles or tanks, guns that could be fired accurately. But tanks weren't suitable for the terrain we were occupying. In the jungle, tanks got tangled up with everything, and they made so much noise you would hear them from a mile away. And rifles weren't large enough for the task at hand. So, taking into account all of these things, I decided to take tank sights and fasten them to the large barrel trajectory guns so they fired in a straight line.

This proved to be very successful. There were lots of mountains in Arakan, and the Japanese had dug tunnels in them. Our troops could take the modified guns and climb the hills very quietly. When they found where the Japanese were based, they were then able to fire the shells straight into the tunnel entrance. We succeeded in capturing more than one hill with these techniques.

This didn't stop me despairing at times at the lack of common sense of some of our men, however. One sergeant major was an example. He got hold of a Japanese hand grenade one afternoon and gathered some of his men around to show them his find. Now Japanese grenades were quite different from our own, where you pulled a ring and there was a delay before they exploded (and you made sure you got rid of them quickly)! The Japanese had to bang their grenades on something hard before they threw them.

I was horrified when this sergeant major put the hand grenade in a vice and then, in a big showmanship gesture, lit a cigarette and put it up to the fuse.

'What are you doing?' I asked.

'Everyone knows that you have to bang a Jap grenade to get it to go off,' he said. 'I'm just showing the boys that these grenades are harmless otherwise. Even a cigarette won't set them off.'

'Well, if you are doing things like that, I'm not staying,' I said, thinking the man was clearly an idiot.

I walked away but hadn't gone very far when there was an explosion behind me. I turned around and the sergeant major and about five men were lying on the ground, all groaning with pain and injured. Thankfully, the grenade must have been defective and it clearly hadn't been full of gunpowder, otherwise they would all be dead. I began to check on them as people came running with medical aid.

There was another sergeant major who was a real nasty individual, a big bullying hulk of a man who also seemed to be lacking common sense. I first encountered him when he came to visit my workshop. He had a water tank that had blocked up – which was a common problem in the jungle conditions – but instead of talking through possible solutions with me, he started abusing the Indian man who was driving the water truck, referring to him as a 'black bastard' and being extremely racist and derogatory. That really made me furious – how dare he talk to another man like that? I gave him a hell of a telling off and told him he should apologise.

Next thing I knew, I was being threatened with a court martial! Later in the day, I was called into a tent with some of the officers, and I knew I was in trouble when I saw their faces. The sergeant major recited his own biased version of events.

'If you ever talk to the sergeant major like that again, we'll have you demoted,' said the officer in charge.

'Well, if he ever talks to any of the Indian men in that way again, I'll bloody well tell him off again,' I retorted.

They seemed surprised that I was standing my ground, but I knew something they didn't. I couldn't be demoted without approval from the War Office because I was a graduate of the Royal Military College of Science. I doubted the sergeant major and his friends would have a leg to stand on trying to present their 'case' to an official board.

I next encountered this sergeant major a couple of weeks later, after a drinking incident. Lord Louis Mountbatten was in charge of the army at that point, and he'd decided that if the sailors could have rum, then the soldiers fighting in the jungle could too. The rum came from Jamaica and was thick like treacle. I didn't drink, but imagined it must have been nearly pure alcohol, looking at the way it stuck like glue to the bottle. It turned out I wasn't the only person who disliked this sergeant major. One of the privates got himself thoroughly drunk one night on Jamaican rum, staggered over to the sergeant major's tent and started shooting. I happened to be walking past with another chap when this happened, so we tackled him and got him to the ground just as he was unhooking a grenade. The private was duly arrested and punished, and the sergeant major survived the attack unscathed and even ended up getting several medals later on. The sergeant major never thanked us for saving his life, and I often wonder about the irony of me being one of the men walking near his tent just as someone with murderous intent was taking shots at him.

I had to wonder about our bad luck and people having no

common sense once again not long after this incident. Another tragedy happened, this time caused by our clunky Sten guns, which were standard fare. The Sten guns looked like something a plumber had made – they were pretty crude – but they were cheap and easy to manufacture. They were nine-millimetre submachine guns that were effective weapons, but they were very temperamental and there was the danger of accidental discharge if the gun was dropped while cocked, because of the firing system. Once it started firing, you couldn't stop it. Several men died when a soldier sat down on his bed, talking to several of his mates, and his Sten gun came off its hook.

Away from these tragedies, I did get to observe some interesting wildlife during this time, which had its own kind of natural drama. I was walking down a narrow jungle trail late one day when a large, exotic cat walked past me. It was twice the size of a domestic cat, and its legs were four times as long. It was very tall and it passed me without making a sound. It wasn't scared of me, but it wasn't aggressive either. Being the curious chap that I am, I followed the cat. It was a light grey colour with dark grey spots. The cat walked down to the water's edge and stood there waiting for the tide to come in before it began scooping fish out. It was an astonishing sight. I found out later that it is called a fishing cat, which is appropriate, and they live in the regions of Pakistan, India, Bangladesh, Arakan, and mainland Southeast Asia. Apparently its closest relative is the leopard. It was a very attractive-looking animal. Unfortunately, I understand they are now an endangered species. Even then, I had a sense they were pretty rare.

Chapter 14
Buthidaung
Apr 1944

In the midst of the jungle, getting fresh water was a problem. Much of the water we had sourced was full of green slime and insects. We had two water trucks, but often the water was so full of insects and gunk the filters got blocked and wouldn't work properly.

We desperately needed to find another water supply, and when I thought about the problem I decided the best course of action was to follow the water up into the mountains. I found a small trickle and tracked it backwards until I found a pond of water. I still remember my delight at the discovery. It was wonderful water – fresh and clear. It had some small shrimps in it, but it was free of other insects, leeches and algae.

I was making my way through the jungle back to camp and I was thinking about the logistics of getting the water tankers close to the pond, given the remoteness of the location, when suddenly a burning liquid hit my arm, covering it from my right hand up to about halfway up my forearm. It was terribly painful, and I noted with alarm that my skin was beginning to come off and hang like a curtain as the liquid flamed and burned. I tried to put the flame out, but it kept burning. It occurred to me that it must be liquid from a flamethrower. I saw no one, and there was no second attempt to kill me.

Somehow I had the energy to run, and when I got to the camp area, I saw a drum of black, used vehicle oil. I knew this would kill the flame, so even though it was filthy, I plunged my arm into it. People came running when they saw what was happening.

'How'd you burn your arm?' asked one of the men.

I couldn't answer him, I was in too much pain, and next I knew someone was administering morphine.

The rest of the evening was a bit of a blur. I remember some men frantically digging a trench nearby as the sun quickly set. A couple of doctors were examining my arm.

'We'll have to operate immediately,' said one.

'But what about lights?' asked the other doctor. 'The sun's almost gone.'

'There are lights... in... my... workshop,' I managed to tell them.

When they understood what I was saying, they sent men to fetch my lights – they were Jeep headlights that ran off batteries, which I had been using to do work at night when required.

I remember the doctors cursing the oil on my arm before I fell into unconsciousness.

When I woke the next day, I was in a forward hospital with about twenty other men in a large tent. They had made a metal frame that suspended my burnt arm, and the doctors explained that after they had removed the loose skin and cleaned everything up, they had sprinkled my burns with sulphanilamide powder, which had only recently been issued to our unit, although I understand it had been around for some time. They then applied ointments and wrapped my arm in cotton wool.

'You're going to have a large scar,' the doctors told me. 'And you won't be able to move any of your fingers from now on. They will close up like a claw.'

I was only a young man, and the thought that I wouldn't be able to have much use of my right hand again was sobering, even for a man who didn't drink.

Later in the day, General Francis Festing came to see me.

'That's a right mess you've made of your arm,' he said, taking a seat by my bed. He looked concerned, and we spoke for a few minutes about what had happened.

'I've been talking to the Americans, and they can get you out on a Duck to an airfield, and we can get you back to India,' General Festing said a little later on.

I struggled to sit a little higher in the bed. 'I don't want to go back. I have too much to do.'

The general gestured at my hand. 'But you can't work with your hand like that.'

'I can use my left hand,' I said, already envisaging how I could continue in my role. 'I'm the only one here who knows how to fix all the instruments – you can't send me back to India when I have a job here to do. It's important I'm on hand to fix urgent repairs and give my men instruction.'

The general looked at me closely, and it seemed he could see I was serious. 'You'll have to stay here until the doctors say you can go back to work,' he said.

I nodded. 'But once I'm recovered sufficiently, I can start teaching other men how to do the work.'

Now it was his turn to nod. 'Well, your team in India is doing a wonderful job, and we do need your expertise here …' His voice trailed off.

'So I can stay?'

'I'll consider it. For now, just concentrate on getting better,' he said.

I stayed in the forward hospital for about a month, bored but happy I was going to be staying and continuing with my work. I think I was as nervous as the doctor looked when he carefully unwound my dressings several weeks on. A thin layer of new skin had grown back – but it seemed to be only one layer, not multiple layers. It hurt to touch anything, but I downplayed the pain, as I was eager to get back to my work.

I couldn't use my right hand properly for several years – and it took eight years for it to finally heal. But I managed to do my work with my left hand and with the help of other men around me. Today, you probably wouldn't be able to tell my hand was injured so badly.

So who had the flamethrower? I've thought about it long and hard ever since, and it seems to me that it wouldn't have been the Japanese, because they would have finished me off. It seems likely it was someone on our side, and that it was an accident they never owned up to. The British Army in Burma didn't have any flamethrowers at that particular time, but I knew the Americans had some in the area we were in. It would seem I was the victim of 'friendly fire'.

And the pond of fresh water I found? The good news was the men back at base camp were still enjoying it.

Chapter 15
Shillong
May – Jul 1944

When I was sufficiently recovered to begin working again, I was posted to Shillong in Assam (which is now part of India). I was delighted to be reunited with my team as we moved the main workshop base from Calcutta to Shillong. The men were in high spirits. Bill was in a very cheery mood, and Munoswami was clearly pleased with our new posting. Nagarajan was all smiles when he saw me. Gabriel was still reserved, but mentioned how good it was to be working directly under my leadership again. Lurdu Swami greeted me like a long-lost friend, his manner typically easy-going and friendly. Dhanaphal was eager to get straight to work, while Kesavan wanted to see our new accommodation first. I had more men in the team too – some I had worked with before; others were new faces. In all, there were about a dozen staff, all ready for the repair work that continued on and on during a war that it seemed would never end.

Shillong was a beautiful place, about six thousand feet above sea level. After the heat of Arakan, it was a climate of contrast. It was very dry and cool, with lovely fresh air and drinking water. It was a desirable location to live, as the climate was so healthy, and it seemed there were more priests there than in all of India and Arakan put together! Away from their religious duties, the priests ran the tea plantations. When we first drove into Shillong, fresh strawberries grew wild in the fields, and I was to learn later the locals also grew a wide variety of vegetables. There was a large Catholic cathedral – a beautiful building with ornate statues – that seemed totally incongruous with the rest of the village, which had elegant but very simple bamboo buildings.

Our accommodation was purpose-built. We had three long army-style buildings to sleep and work in. Once again, we quickly settled into a productive work routine, and I supervised what everyone was doing. My burnt hand was giving me a lot of problems, and it took me months to just hold a pen, but I kept myself useful by taking charge of the team. I eventually learnt to write with my left hand. It never occurred to me that I should have gone into an Indian hospital and then back to England. I wanted to be useful to the war effort, and I wanted to stay where I could help the most.

It didn't take us long to meet the local Khasi people. They reminded me of photographs I have seen of the Sherpas of Nepal. They were small but strong people and they were always joking and laughing. They had a culture where the men played cards all day and the women did all the work. They also had an accepted culture where a man could have a wife in town and then another in the one of the remote villages – and the same was accepted for the women as well – so most adults had two mates.

The local women used to come and see us once a day, and they provided us with firewood. The women would load what looked like large ice cream cones on their backs with firewood and tramp across the hills to us without seeming to be bothered by the hard physical work. They always appeared in a large group, with the younger women accompanied by older relatives, and they usually had their babies in tow as well.

The women were extremely outgoing and spoke good English. They used to love to chew betel nuts, which contains chemicals that are similar to nicotine. The betel nut would stain their mouths bright red. They were always trying to convince me to try chewing the betel nuts, but I never did.

The Khasi women were incredibly hard-working and fun-loving people. Everybody wanted a Khasi woman as a live-in housekeeper. I often used to ask if I could take their photograph, but they were very afraid of them. They were worried that if I printed the photographs, someone would then put pinholes in them and they would get ill, sort of like a voodoo thing. I got around this by saying I would be in the photograph with them, and that seemed to solve the problem.

My men were working two twelve-hour shifts at this stage, six days a week. I worked eighteen hours, six days a week, so I spent nine hours of each shift with my men. We were repairing about two hundred binoculars a week, which was an admirable feat. When they were repaired, they looked as good as new; the only thing we didn't do was paint them. We also repaired compasses, which mostly involved putting new seals on them and getting the bubbles out of the liquid by placing the compass in a vacuum. It was a busy time. I used to have Saturdays off, so when several of the local people invited me to come and see their village at Happy Valley – and agreed I could take photographs – I accepted their invitation, curious to learn more about these industrious people.

A group of about five women turned up on Saturday to guide me to their village, laughing and joking as they walked ahead.

'How far away is your village?' I asked as we set off.

'Not far,' they told me. 'You'll be back soon.'

Thinking their village was probably only a few hundred yards away, I was happy to follow them. We entered a lush and beautiful valley, and then, to my astonishment, the women began climbing up a very tall waterfall, nimbly moving from stone to stone without any trouble. They gestured for me to follow, and that's when I realised how fit these women really were. It was incredibly hard work climbing the waterfall, and I was risking a nasty thirty-foot fall. I was utterly exhausted and out of breath by the time I got to the top. It would appear that the high altitude was taking its toll on me!

Several of them approached me on the trip and asked if I would 'stay' with them but I quickly declined.

'Why do you want me to stay with you?' I asked one of them, curiosity winning out over discretion in the end.

'Because you have healthy red cheeks and I'd like a child with red cheeks,' she said. 'Don't you like me?' she added.

'You're very nice,' I said. 'But I can't be with a woman who chews betel nuts,' thinking that would end the conversation while I reflected that the cold temperatures must be making my cheeks red.

'Oh, I'll stop,' she promptly said.

'But what about your husband?'

'He's fighting with the Gurkhas. I don't know where he is,' she replied. 'I'm sure he'll be back sometime.'

She didn't seem worried about him, and I somehow managed to extricate myself from this conversation that had suddenly veered off course.

Eventually we got to their small village via a long path. It turned out I was now about eight miles away from Shillong, although it felt like I'd walked much further. I was incredibly thirsty when I arrived, and I asked if I could have some water. They pointed to a bucket and some fresh-looking water that was coming out of a piece of bamboo. I eagerly filled my bucket with water, but then, to my horror, I found I didn't have the strength to lift it!

Unfortunately, the women found this incredibly funny, and much to my embarrassment, they started giggling and laughing. I didn't really know what to do at that point, but eventually the moment passed and someone helped me with the water. I felt even more embarrassed when I noticed the work many of the women were doing. Older Khasi women were breaking up large rocks, while young Khasi women were breaking the larger rocks into small pieces of gravel with hammers. They then loaded the small rocks into their cone backpacks, which must have been a really heavy load, and walked away into the distance. I found out they were building a nearby road entirely by hand – and I couldn't even lift a bucket of water!

They were incredibly hospitable, however. There were only a few buildings, but they showed me to a bamboo barn that was filled with sweetcorn and potatoes and all sorts of lovely fresh vegetables, all smoked to preserve them. I couldn't help but notice how happy everyone was. They really had the most basic type of accommodation and possessions – they practically had nothing – but each of them was genuinely happy with their lot in life. It seemed appropriate that the place was called Happy Valley.

There were no men to be seen, except for the brother of one of the women. I was told the other men were playing cards in one of the buildings. The man I met was only small, but he was carrying the most enormous bag of potatoes. He had material around his forehead that went under the huge sack of potatoes that was strapped to his back. He was so strong they showed me a photograph of him carrying a grand piano on his back. I was amazed that such small people could carry such heavy loads.

I was offered some food, although I was so exhausted I could barely eat, and a young, very nice-looking woman sat next to me.

'I want to sleep with you,' she said.

I explained that wasn't going to happen, but she didn't seem too put off by my reply. We got talking about her life there, and she had a good-looking seven-year-old son who could also speak very good English. I was a little surprised when I learnt that she was still breastfeeding him, but he was a very fine young boy.

By now the sun had set, and I realised that I needed to stay overnight, so accommodation was found for me, a building that was clean and tidy and well kept. It had a very comfortable bed with starched white sheets and pillowcases – just like a hotel. After the day's exertions, I quickly fell into a deep sleep.

When I woke in the morning, I was surprised to find the woman whom I'd spoken to last night in bed with me. Needless to say, the entire situation was very awkward. I got up and told her I had to get back to my base camp. I was well aware that the local women had a 'free' approach to their relationships, and if they were of a certain age, they could proactively choose the men they wanted to sleep with. But I wasn't keen. It had been drilled into us not to have casual encounters like this. She didn't seem bothered by my insistence that I had to go.

Needless to say, it had been a very interesting interlude, and I still remember my time at Happy Valley fondly.

Chapter 16
Tinsukia
Aug 1944

It was back when my workshop was based in Poona that I first heard of something almost mythical – that there was allegedly an air-conditioned army workshop based in Tinsukia. I met a young lieutenant who said he had been there and that it was wonderful.

I was excited when I was able to go and see the fabled Tinsukia for myself. The village was only a small place with a handful of bamboo-constructed buildings that serviced the needs of the local tea growers, but what a sight the workshop was! It was a newly constructed two-storey circular building that looked a little like a large temple. Next to it was a building that repaired army vehicles. It had top-quality lino floors and everything was immaculate. It was a very impressive facility and, at the time, something quite out of this world. It was just what we needed to service precision technical devices.

I was curious to know how such a state-of-the-art building came to be in such a remote location, and I found the answers when I got into a conversation with the English sergeant major who was in charge of the workshop, whose official rank was that of conductor.

'I was in England at the time of Dunkirk, and the British Army lost most of their technical people at that time,' he said. 'They convinced me that I should train as an instrument person, although I didn't know anything about instruments. But they sent me on a course and then sent me to India to do the job.'

He sighed and ran a hand through his thinning hair. 'Unfortunately, even after doing the course, I still didn't know anything about repairing instruments, so I just told them I couldn't work because of the conditions – that it was too hot and humid to do repair work.'

He frowned. 'I thought that would get them off my back and I could go and do something else, but they built this air-conditioned building and now I'm stuck here.' Showing me around the facility, he brought my attention to stockpiles of instruments that were waiting for repair. There were typewriters and gun sights, compasses and binoculars. He was a very pleasant man in his middle years, but he looked sheepish when revealing the extent of his failure. He hadn't touched any of the instruments; instead, he spent his time assisting the motor mechanics. It was clear he was a victim of the fast-tracking that the war casualties had caused for some men – people thrust into technical roles they were unsuited for.

'I can help you with all of this,' I said, and he immediately looked brighter. 'I'll get started on the more difficult repairs, and I'll get my team in here to finish off everything else.'

I was only in Tinsukia for a few weeks, but I thoroughly enjoyed my time there. I had plenty of work to keep me occupied, and I was pleased my team would have such a wonderful facility to work from. Before my team arrived, I spent time training other Indian men how to repair instruments. I always ran the workshop as though everyone was my mate, and that seemed to encourage very high standards in the men I trained. It was very satisfying work.

But I did notice not everyone was as content as I was. Admittedly it was a very hot and humid climate, and away from work there was nothing much to do and nowhere to go. Seven of the sergeant majors, including the sergeant major in charge of the workshop, devised a drinking game which they played most evenings. They used to go to their non-commissioned officers' mess, a large building built of bamboo, and sit in seven soft armchairs that they had arranged in a circle on the mud floor. Of course, in that climate there were lots of insects and lizards. At night-time, the men lit pressurised kerosene lamps that attracted the insects. Dazzled, the creatures would hit the light and then fall from the ceiling to the ground. I don't know which of the men came up with the idea, but each of them 'owned' a toad and a gecko. They would place the lizards on the wall and the toads on the floor, and whoever's creature caught an insect first would pay for the next round of drinks. So that's what they did each night – when they weren't working in the workshop, they were sitting in their armchairs, drinking Indian gin and watching the insects. It just shows you what some people will do for amusement in the jungle!

When I wasn't working, I spent time looking around the local countryside, a prosperous tea-planting area. Indian women worked the fields, which were usually owned by wealthy European men. They used to pick the green leaves and throw the leaves into a container on their backs, and when their containers were full, they would pour the leaves onto flat concrete to dry in the sun. In a couple of days, the tea was black, and they packed it in silver-lined boxes to go to Europe. I still remember how good that tea tasted – much better than standard army fare! On one occasion, the Indian women were getting very nervous about working in the fields as there was a leopard prowling around. The Indian foreman got a bamboo pole, sharpened it to a point and promised the women that he would protect them. It all came to a head one night when there was a lot of noise coming from the chickens at the back of his house. He went into their hut, lashed out with a knife and killed the leopard. I guess it was good the leopard wasn't endangering the women, but it did seem a sad end to such a noble beast.

While I was there, the locals caught a king cobra that was about six metres long – the ordinary cobras were only about a metre long. It was an astonishingly large snake and one that was highly poisonous.

By then, my time at Tinsukia was at an end. Munoswami and my team were on their way, and I had new orders. This time I was going to Burma.

Chapter 17
Digboi and Samaw
Sep 1944

In September, I had orders to join the headquarters of the 36th Division, who were now in Samaw, Burma. I was to leave most of my staff at the workshop in Tinsukia, but I was able to take five men with me. I chose the fittest and brightest Indian men from my team to accompany me. I'm not sure what they thought about going into Burma, away from the relative safety they had enjoyed at Poona, Calcutta and Tinsukia, but they all followed me without hesitation. And I was pleased to have these fine young men with me – Nagarajan, who was the brightest in my team, Lurdu Swami, the most easy-going, Dhanaphal, who was an incredibly hard worker, Gabriel, who was the most courteous of men, and Kesavan, who was a fine all-rounded individual. They would be my closest companions in the months ahead.

It was arranged that the Americans would take us into Burma. I had a Jeep and a trailer that we loaded with workshop tools and equipment, and we drove to Ledo airfield, just out of Digboi.

It proved to be a long trip. We were travelling on a makeshift road that was only wide enough for one truck. A convoy of American trucks came towards us from the opposite direction, and the first driver deliberately ran me off the road into the swamp. I was furious, and my men were trying to push us out of a swamp when another American driver stopped and pulled us out – grudgingly, without talking to us. We had only travelled a few miles when another American truck drove us off the road, and then a little later another American driver pulled us out of the swamp again – once again, he was surly and uncommunicative.

'This is ridiculous!' said Kesavan the third time we were run off the road by an American driver. 'We're supposed to be on the same side!'

I realise American soldiers have a reputation for being friendly, but I have to say from my experiences they weren't friendly to us in that part of the world. A heck of a lot of them had a very low opinion of the British and Indian armies. And with these shenanigans we were late getting to the airfield.

Ledo was a very primitive airfield. It was situated halfway up a mountain, and some trees had been cut down and ground levelled to create a very basic runway. It was an airfield that we could only use in the dry season, when the ground was rock hard, because in the monsoon season everything turned to mud.

It was getting dark when we arrived, and it was clear when the American pilot came out to greet us that he was in hurry to get going. He asked me to load my Jeep and trailer, as though this were something I did every day. Of course, this was the first time I'd done it, but with my men's help, I drove the Jeep onto the loading ramp and then spent some time trying to work out how the hooks and wires in the plane worked so the load was securely fastened. I had expected the pilot to come back and see if we had done everything correctly, but instead, before we had a chance to catch our breath, the plane was hurtling down the runway. There weren't any seats, so each of us stood holding onto the wire that hung from the plane's ceiling. As the plane shuddered upward, the pilot yelled for me to come up front, so I ended up standing behind his seat as he flew. Beside him were two other Americans, but they didn't pay me any attention.

'Crikey,' said the pilot, 'what have you got back there? It was just a Jeep and an empty trailer, wasn't it?"

At that moment, the wheels on the plane clipped the tops of the trees at the end of the runway, making a terrible racket.

'They're full of instruments,' I shouted over the din.

'Instruments?'

'Workshop tools and materials,' I shouted. 'It's a heavy load.'

'You could say that again. I thought they were empty,' the pilot said.

He managed to pull the plane up, just above the level of the trees. I was amazed to see that he didn't look too bothered that we were struggling to get altitude with the load. Instead, he reached into his shirt pocket and handed me a photograph. It was an image of a young woman with long dark hair and sparkling eyes.

'I'm planning on meeting her real soon,' he said.

I wasn't sure if she was his sweetheart or what the story was. 'That sounds good,' I eventually said.

He gestured for me to hand the photo back. 'She sure is a honey,' he said. 'You know, I've just turned twenty-one, but I figure I'll be done with this war soon.'

'How's that?'

'Every flight we do counts as points, and when I have enough points, I'll be going home.'

I considered this and realised now, with this new information, why they were so keen to give us a lift – it was a completely different situation for our British pilots and us, who were stuck here for the duration.

We were now at the top of the mountain, but to my increasing alarm I noticed we were only just skimming across the top of the rocks. The pilot cursed under his breath and turned his attention back to his flying. It was clear he couldn't get enough altitude because of the weight we were carrying. I was annoyed once again that he hadn't come to check the load before taking off.

It was a perilous, heart-palpitating flight as the plane rose and fell, often perilously close to the rocks below. It seemed every time we got to a flat part of rock, the plane got a bit of altitude, but as soon as we were past, the plane dropped again. I looked out the window. The rocks were capped in snow and it was too cold for anything to grow. I looked back at my men, and they all looked nervous. I nodded at them in a way that I hoped would cause them to feel more confident, but who was I kidding? Our fate was in the hands of a talkative, over-confident, gung-ho twenty-one-year-old pilot.

We had been travelling for about an hour when we came to a forest, and I simply hoped the pilot would keep us above the treeline. That's when I looked down and saw the wreck of another plane that had crashed into the forest, carving out a trail of destruction in its path. The pilot flew through the gap in the trees the crashed plane had carved out, and then we saw the most astonishing sight. High up in the jungle, we were suddenly looking into a large tree hut, and around a dozen local people stared at us with wide eyes as we flew past at their level. I don't know who was more surprised, us or them!

I felt very relieved when the pilot announced we would be landing. He'd spotted an airfield, and he circled down low for a landing that was bumpy but finally had us on terra firma.

'Well,' he said to me as he turned his engines off. 'I'd expected to be at least a hundred feet higher on that trip, but we're here in one piece, so that's good news.'

'And where are we exactly?'

We both peered out into the darkness. It was now pitch black. He shrugged. 'It's not Myitkyina, but this will do for the night.'

The pilot and his silent companions disappeared, while my men and I decided we'd sleep in the Jeep. We couldn't put our lights on as there could be Japanese around, but we managed to get the Jeep and trailer unloaded, and we found a place to park surrounded by trees. It was horribly cold, but we survived the night intact. When we woke, the plane had gone again, and it seemed we were completely on our own. We drove for a little bit and discovered an empty camp. It looked quite eerie – rows of tents with beds ready but no one there. We rested there for a while but decided we had to move on, especially as there was no food or water.

'I wonder where we are?' said Kesavan.

I shrugged, not wanting to say we were lost and I had no means of communication with anyone because we didn't have a radio.

'I think we should follow those vehicle tracks,' I said. 'I'm sure we'll be in Myitkyina soon.'

'Excellent idea,' said Kesavan.

We followed the vehicle tracks until we happened across a railway line. We got out of the Jeep and looked at the line. It stretched as far as the eye could see from north to south.

'This looks promising,' said Nagarajan after a time.

I followed his gaze and could see a train in the distance heading our way. As it got closer, I could see it was an engine that was towing what we called 'flats' – that is, platforms with wheels. Two Americans were towing the flats, and they slowed and stopped when they saw us.

'Where are you headed?' the taller of the two asked.

'Myitkyina,' I said.

He threw back his head and laughed. 'You're about two hundred miles from there.'

'So where's the nearest town?'

'Samaw,' he replied. 'We're going south.'

'Can you take us there?'

'Sure thing. Load your vehicles and we'll get going.'

I looked at my men, but they were already running to the Jeep.

'One more thing,' the man said.

'What's that?'

He eyed the weapons I was wearing. 'If anyone tries to stop the train, just shoot them.'

We loaded everything onto the flats and then got behind the end flat and helped push it. The flats alone weighed tonnes, so it took a while for us to pick up any speed. The steel wheels made sparks on the track and eventually we jumped on board. We had been travelling for some time, and I estimated we were probably doing about sixty miles an hour, when we spotted a herd of water buffalos. They were large, almost as big as elephants, magnificent-looking beasts totally comfortable in their surroundings. But then I noticed one of the buffalos was standing on the railway tracks ahead of us. I had a sick feeling realising we wouldn't be able to stop in time, and even though the driver began to break, it was a terrible sound when we hit the animal. The train eventually stopped and we got out. The poor animal had all its legs broken, and the driver was emptying ammunition into the beast to kill it.

It seemed to take ages to die, this huge water buffalo, and I think we all felt ill that it was suffering before it finally passed. My men looked as grim as I felt when we helped drag the animal off the tracks, and we were all sombre when we continued on our way.

We finally arrived at our destination. Samaw was a small village surrounded by dense jungle and next to a very steep volcanic-style mountain. We soon learnt that the Japanese had extensively tunnelled it and were making a nuisance of themselves in the area. We met a group of Merrill's Marauders there, American soldiers that were becoming famous for their deep-penetration missions fighting the Japanese in Burma.

The captain there was in charge of about fifty men, and they were discussing the Japanese up in the mountains.

'Look, you guys, we are going up that hill and we are going to get those Japs,' said the captain.

'You and who else?' asked one of the men, a large, strapping soldier.

The captain didn't reply, and I was amazed a soldier was talking back to a captain in that way, but it was clear from the attitude of the men they had had enough of Japanese tunnels for the time being, and no one went up the mountain while we were there. For a moment I wanted to volunteer, but I realised that would be extremely foolhardy. Instead, I got my men to set up camp. Tomorrow we would worry about what we were going to do next. In the meantime, my pressing concern was getting us some supplies. We had nothing to eat and only a small supply of water left.

I approached the Americans and asked if we could have some of their K-rations, but they replied they only had enough for themselves. Hungry and a feeling a little angry, I went to bed that night and contemplated the situation. We were a couple of hundred miles from where we were supposed to be, in the middle of a dense jungle, surrounded by hostile Japanese troops who were hiding out in well-fortified tunnels. We had no food, and apart from the Americans we had met who had given us a ride on the flats, the other American soldiers were just out-and-out unfriendly. Our welcome to Burma wasn't what I had hoped. We were there to repair instruments, but I could see our first priority was something else – survival.

Chapter 18
Samaw
Sept 1944

I repeatedly asked the Americans if we could have some of their food, and they repeatedly told me they couldn't spare any rations, as they only had enough for themselves. I didn't believe them. I had never seen so much food stockpiled, all in their neat, tidy, rectangular boxes. That's when I decided we'd have to steal what we needed. I had already observed where their food stores were hidden, so I waited until it was dark and slid under the barbed wire fence into the American's area. I pushed the food parcels under the barbed wire to my Indian men and they loaded the supplies into the Jeep. Simple!

We sped along the dirt tracks and then stopped when the camp was out of sight and had a feast, enjoying the tinned fruit, currants, biscuits and Spam.

'This tastes especially good,' said Lurdu Swami, tucking into a tin of peaches.

'It certainly does,' agreed Gabriel, munching on some biscuits.

We set up camp for the night and in the morning headed off, our destination Myitkyina, where headquarters at that time were based. We hadn't gone very far when two Chindits stepped out from the dense jungle, waving us down. These British Army soldiers were part of a special elite force trained to operate behind Japanese lines, but these particular two men were in very bad shape. We gave them some food and water and they told us their story.

'We were flown in but we crash-landed,' said the taller of the two.

His hands shook as he drank from the water bottle I gave him, and he looked feverish and ill with malaria.

'We got lost and haven't seen anyone for days,' said the other man.

'Where are your weapons?' asked Nagarajan.

'We ran out of bullets,' said the tall man, and he shrugged. He didn't need to explain that they had thrown their weapons away. 'I don't suppose you have a radio?' he added.

'Sorry, you know how it is,' I replied.

The truth was very few people had access to radios in the jungle. In those days, the radios were large, in thick suitcases and incredibly heavy, so the men carrying them had to be really strong. And that aside, the army just didn't have enough radios to go around everyone.

'But I do have working compasses and maps, so we'll get you to the nearest camp,' I said.

I spread the maps I had on the Jeep bonnet so they could see where they were going, and then we gave them a lift up the road to the nearest British Army camp. They urgently needed food and medical attention, and I could see they wouldn't be getting that from the nearby American base. I gave them a compass when we parted and thought how important it was to have a working compass in the jungle. I prided myself on making sure that any compasses I repaired were in perfect working order. They could be tricky to repair, as bubbles in the liquid could make them stick, but there was a technique of holding them still for a time until they settled down.

We were now in a part of the country where they grew sugar cane, and we came across a building that used to be part of the local sugar company. They had one or two nice bungalows there and no sign of anybody occupying them. We found a storeroom with field lights that were used for surveying, all smashed. I don't know why these lights had been smashed; it seemed such a waste, especially as we were in an area where in ten minutes, daylight turned to dark. We decided to stay to do some repairs, and I organised some lights for the bungalows, but of course this only attracted the insects. When dusk fell, we were all working inside the building, and within a few minutes all our work desks were covered in white flies, almost like a covering of snow. We obviously couldn't continue our repairs with all those insects, so we gave up at that stage, turned off our lights and went to bed.

We finished the repairs in the morning and then travelled for several days, making our way south of Mytikyina without further incident. But when our supplies had run out, I found I had a craving for eggs. We stopped in a small village and split up to explore. I was walking along a small track when a scruffy-looking young Burmese man came walking towards me, followed by a couple of local women.

'Hello,' I said to him in what I hoped was passable Burmese.

He stopped and stared at me.

'Do you have any eggs?' I asked in Burmese.

He frowned and gestured that he couldn't understand me.

I tried again in a number of different Indian dialects, but he continued to look perplexed. The women behind him huddled close to him and looked confused. Suddenly inspired, I grabbed up a stick, drew the outline of a chicken in the sand and made clucking noises like a hen.

The young man nodded and the women giggled. Encouraged, I made some more clucking noises.

'Do you speak English?' asked the man with a smile, in perfect English.

I stared at him, amazed. 'I certainly can, but – but where did you learn to speak English?'

'My father is a professor,' he replied. 'Now, what is it you want?'

'Eggs,' I said, feeling very silly after my recent performance. 'Um, do you have any eggs that my men and I could eat?'

'We don't have edible eggs, but we can give you some eggs that are ready to hatch.'

He gestured for me to follow, and he took me to where some chickens were housed. The chickens in Burma were several times bigger than English chickens, and their cockerels were trained to fight and had extra horns on the back of their legs. I was pleased not to get close to them. The man gave me half a dozen eggs and a hen, for which I thanked him gratefully. I got back to my men, and they were in fits of laughter when I regaled them with my meeting and language difficulties.

I built a chicken house and attached it to one of the trucks, and we continued on our journey. Just out of the village, we came across several drainage creeks the size of a man. I noticed they were full of strange-looking creature that looked like a cross between a crocodile and a fish. They had a long head with teeth that looked just like crocodile teeth, but they had bodies shaped like fish. We stopped to investigate further, caught some of them and cooked them up. They were extremely tasty.

Several days later, we were closer to our destination, but once again hungry and without food. Some of the chickens had hatched, but they weren't big enough to eat, so I decided it was time to take action. While my men were having a well-deserved rest, I crafted fishing hooks out of builder's nails, some tough line and some bait – in this case, a small piece of leftover 'crocodile' fish. I headed down the bank to the nearby river and found what looked like a good spot for fishing. It was a fast-flowing river, and it was clear a bomb had fallen, creating a crater in the river deeper than normal. I had been there for about half an hour when I felt a pull on the line, but the fish must have been a large one because I couldn't pull it ashore.

It was a hot, humid day after lots of monsoon rain, so I reset my bait and began to fish again. I had been told that in this part of the country in future months the rivers would dry up until they were just mud, and the local people would go to the wettest parts to reach in and pull out the fish. But there was still plenty of water in the river then, so I continued fishing the time-honoured, traditional way.

It was peaceful. The only sound was the buzz of tropical insects – until the sound of gunfire split the air. Instinct took over as I dived behind a fallen tree, realising as I did that Japanese were firing on me. I looked around, my heart pounding loudly. My only escape was up a very steep bank – but I realised my chances of running up that bank and getting away were nil. There appeared to be about six or seven Japanese firing at me, and my only consolation in this life-threatening situation was that they were situated on the other side of the river.

It was precarious being outnumbered like this, but I found I was surprisingly calm. The firing seemed to go on incessantly, but I had no intention of firing my own weapons. If I did, it would immediately confirm I was in the British Army, and it would give my position away. If I had to use my bullets, I would save them until the enemy was closer. I was just thinking about my different options, of which admittedly I had very few, when I heard another noise coming in the opposite direction. It was the sound of marching. I took a chance and peered over the fallen tree up the bank, and the sight that greeted me cheered me considerably. There were about thirty Chinese soldiers marching past, their guns at the ready. They must have heard the Japanese firing at me and come to investigate. Moments later, they began firing into the bush across the river, and the Japanese stopped shooting straight away. I made my escape up the bank and to safety.

As I made my way back to my men, I reflected that I hadn't succeeded in catching any fish and we were likely to go hungry for the night, but at least I was alive. That had been a close call.

Chapter 19
Myitkyina
Oct 1944

It didn't take long to settle into a routine south of Myitkyina. We spent our days repairing instruments, working long shifts to get through the workload. General Francis Festing came to talk to me during this time when he wanted something fixed, and I thoroughly enjoyed our conversations. We mainly talked about the work I was doing, what I needed and how we were managing – and our conversation was always easy. I always had his watches and pipes to repair. He was a really nice man, intelligent, level-headed, good at listening and full of common sense. We used to call him 'Front-Line Frankie' as an affectionate nickname.

My team and I were so busy we didn't have time for chit-chat, however, and we always discouraged visitors. Occasionally I would have some young officer turn up making a nuisance of themselves, probably suspicious that I had a self-contained unit of men working independently from everyone, the only unit of its kind in the Burmese jungle – and perhaps anywhere in the world – but they were usually easy to get rid of when they discovered that I only took orders from the general's senior appointed staff.

I read a little during this period in my rare spare time. I used to put fireflies in my torch, in front of the reflector. This allowed for a strange flashing light that provided enough illumination to read by. I was quickly getting used to the different sounds of the Burmese jungle, although many of the sounds used to drive some of the other soldiers up the wall. There was a 'knock-knock' sound that seemed to occur nightly. Many of the men were convinced it was the sound of Japanese tapping bamboo to signal to each other. I was determined to discover what it really was, so one day I got myself a white sheet and boiled it with leaves and dirt to camouflage it. I dug myself a shallow space to sleep in, near where I had heard the 'knock-knock' noise before, and then pulled the sheet across the top of me and bent it back so I could just see past the edge. That night, I watched the bushes carefully, listening to the now-familiar noise. I was lying there when a bird flew up into the night, and I knew straight away from the way it flew and from the shape of its wings it was an owl. One landed on my camouflaged mosquito net another night; it was smaller than a European barn owl but much bigger than a New Zealand morepork.

Another time, some soldiers were convinced they could hear the marching of Japanese soldiers, but I discovered this sound was actually large ants. Some people were really going quite mad in the jungle with the different sounds, and they believed any rumour that was circulating, rather than trying to identify the cause of the noises.

There was another noise that sounded like terrible swearing, like someone saying a particular word over and over. Nobody knew what was causing it. It always started when it got dark, and it never happened during daylight. I was determined to find out the cause, so I made a note of where the sound came from. I found a deep crack in a big tree, but there was nothing in the crack that I could see in the daylight. At night-time, I investigated further, and, sure enough, the sound of swearing was coming from this tree. When I shone my torch in the crack, there was a huge grey lizard. It looked like it was blowing up a balloon, and then, when the air escaped, it made a noise like it was swearing. It sounded very rude, and it was nearly a metre long! But it was good to assure everybody it was just a lizard.

I was also intrigued by the flying stick insects no thicker than my finger that made a clattering noise when they flew but didn't appear to have any wings.

Mosquitoes were always a problem in the jungle conditions. I reflected that the Japanese were actually smarter than us when it came to insect protection. They had cloth wrapped around their legs that prevented insects biting them. Our trousers didn't stop them and we didn't have any insect repellent, so it was up to every man to cope as best as he could. I used to cover myself with Vaseline to create a barrier on my skin. It seemed to help. Leeches were a problem too – they would attach themselves to you without you realising. They'd be the size of a matchstick to begin with, but when they'd sucked enough blood, they were as big as two thumbs put together.

One incident during this time sticks in my mind. I was outdoors late one day after a long shift when I turned slightly and saw the most extraordinary sight. A large tiger, much bigger than any tiger I have ever seen in a zoo, suddenly walked out of the jungle to my right. I froze, holding my breath, willing myself not to make a sound. The tiger was fiercely beautiful and it moved with a sleek motion, its muscles rippling beneath its fur, its tail swinging. It opened its mouth wide and roared, a loud, wild sound that gave me goosebumps. My heart was racing, although I felt calm, and then the creature turned and disappeared back into the foliage. What a magnificent sight!

My normal work was put on hold one day when General Festing came to my workshop with an unusual problem.

'The Chinese general gave me a gift last night,' he said, puffing on his pipe. 'I'll have to return the favour. Any suggestions?'

I stared at him for a moment. We were in the middle of a jungle and there were certainly no shops where we were.

'I guess I could make something,' I said slowly, an idea already coming to me.

'I'd appreciate that, Hennessy,' said the general. 'I thought you'd be the man to help me out.'

I got to work immediately, leaving my men to continue on with the usual instrument repairs. I used the covers of shell caps, which were made of brass, melted them down and then fashioned them in the shape of wine goblets. I asked a Chinese soldier I knew to write down the symbols for 'good luck', and I engraved the Chinese wording on them. Then I made some lacquer from tree sap diluted with methylated spirits. To finish off, I made a casket out of wood from the jungle to house the six goblets. In all, this took about a week from start to finish. The finished result looked surprisingly good, and when I showed them to the general he was very pleased. I was very pleased too. I had crafted a quality gift from only what was available to me in the jungle. Other people would have said it couldn't be done, but I had enjoyed the challenge.

Unfortunately, the old saying that pride comes before a fall proved to be true. I found out the next day that all the generals had gathered together and the gift had been presented. They had filled the goblets with strong alcohol and then raised their glasses in a toast. Unfortunately, when they went to drink, their lips stuck to the goblets! The alcohol had melted the lacquer! It never occurred to me they might actually use them – I expected them to only be used as ornaments. Fortunately, everyone saw the funny side of the incident, and it didn't cause any problems.

I soon had other things to occupy my mind. The general wanted my team on the road, behind enemy lines, to repair instruments for the various units. We were set to go travelling again.

Chapter 20
Hopin
Nov 1944

By this stage of the war, I felt a bit like Robin Hood travelling with his merry men. General Festing gave us instructions to travel to various destinations in Burma. I was given a map and told to drive so many miles east or west, and then we would set up base in a village. Sometimes we found buildings where we could do our repair work, but more often than not we worked out of our vehicles and slept outdoors. We travelled with our two three-tonne army trucks, and I had attached a bath to one of the trucks so we could keep clean. We also travelled with the chicken coop and rice to feed the chickens for a time, but we soon got rid of them. They were all fighting birds and made so much noise they were proving to be a dangerous liability. We eventually abandoned any hope of keeping the hens for fresh eggs and ate them instead.

We often had no food supplies so had to turn to the land to support us. When we were lucky, we found wild chillies to make curries, and I used to do a lot of fishing. We didn't have a radio, so communication was difficult. But we managed to repair a lot of instruments for the troops in the area during this time, so we were all aware we were making a difference to the war effort.

It was a great adventure, although I was always conscious that we were in dangerous territory. The British and the Indians wanted to kill the Japanese. The Americans wanted to kill the Japanese. The Chinese wanted to kill the Japanese. I didn't particularly want to kill anyone, but I knew for sure that the Japanese would want to kill me. As for the Burmese, they were neutral in all of this and didn't have any weapons, although they had all these other people in the country fighting each other. They didn't like the Japanese – they made sure they didn't upset them, but you could tell they were very unhappy with the situation. Many of them were religious and didn't believe in killing anything, even a fly, rat or snake.

In this situation, I was extra careful with our sleeping arrangements, and my men were happy to follow my lead. We used to cut bits of bamboo, make both ends sharp and jam them into the ground on an angle to make it difficult for any enemy troops lurking in the jungle. It was a barrier that made it tricky for them to get past. We put stones in tins on a string and attached them to the bamboo stakes, knowing this would wake us up if we were approached by anyone. I didn't have a problem sleeping taking these precautions.

We always stopped when it was dark when we were making our way along the jungle tracks. We wouldn't lie down to sleep unless it was dark, just in case the Japanese could see us. On one occasion, we found a comfortable piece of ground that wasn't too hard or rocky. We smoothed the leaves, and, after taking all the usual precautions, we settled in for the night. We always slept in pairs, and on this night I was sharing my space with Lurdu Swami. We both woke up in puzzlement in the middle of the night when we felt something moving underneath us. It was too dark to see anything except the whites of Lurdu Swami's eyes.

'Do you feel that?' he whispered.

'Yes.'

'What do you think it is?' he asked.

'I don't know. Some creature, I think, but it's not attacking us, so let's wait until daylight to investigate.'

'Okay.'

He began to close his eyes, and I was impressed with his nonchalant attitude. There were many men who wouldn't have been so relaxed in this unknown situation, but he must have come to the same conclusion as I had – whatever was happening, we weren't in any immediate danger.

I fell into an uneasy sleep and woke at first light. The movement had stopped, but I woke just in time to see a huge king cobra disappearing into the jungle. I realised with a flash of insight we had spent some of the night resting on this huge creature, and we had probably disturbed its nest! Lurdu Swarmi looked both relieved and alarmed when I told him – relieved there was now no danger but alarmed because he was nervous of snakes.

The next day, we were travelling and came to a grove of very tall trees by a river. It was a nice day, so after we had got through the day's work, I decided to have a break. I tied the waterproof cloth we used at night-time to two trees to create a hammock. I was just lying there relaxing when I looked up and noticed a bird's nest, so I decided to climb up the tree to see what type of bird was there. What a mistake that was! When I reached out, I discovered the nest didn't contain a bird but instead red ants! They had heads with pincers that stuck to my body, and in seconds I was covered in a swarm of ants. I scuttled down the tree and jumped into the river to get rid of them. I literally had hundreds of bites.

I was just finishing drying myself off when I looked up to see the most curious sight. A black bird dive-bombed the nest, breaking it into pieces. It deliberately wiggled around, and, within seconds, it was covered in ants. It flew off eating the ants, and I marvelled that at that moment a black bird had turned brilliant red!

I was still itchy and a little irritable several nights later when we arrived at a place called Hopin. We had only been there a short time when I noticed that every evening as the sun was setting, the wind blew through the trees and we could hear the sound of bells. It was a beautiful, slightly eerie sound deep in the Burmese jungle. The men and I discussed it and decided we would go and investigate.

We walked into the jungle in the direction we had heard the bells and came across a most incongruous sight. We discovered a large temple that looked like it had been there for hundreds, if not thousands, of years. It was a very large temple, whereas most of the other temples we had discovered previously were small and usually full of spiders, lizards and snakes. This was a large, imposing building that looked Greek in origin. I wondered if it was a temple that Alexander the Great could have been responsible for creating. We stood and stared in amazement for a moment. Surrounding this rectangular temple were dried-up rose gardens – a most curious thing to find in a tropical jungle.

'Let's have a look,' I said eventually.

We walked towards the large teak doors and stepped inside the temple. Carefully looking around the inside of the temple, we saw it seemed to have been used as some kind of museum. There was a lot of broken glass and it was clear that some of the exhibits had been removed, but there were carvings, bronze statues and paintings of animals that were probably long extinct. There were about twenty large handmade, hand-written books. There was a large Buddha on a huge plate supported by thirty carved ivory elephants. The Buddha was solid gold and the biggest Buddha I have ever seen. I estimate it was probably about twelve metres high.

Also inside the temple was a glass pagoda that was covered in gold leaf in the shape of ivy creepers, with Chinese-style curled-edged framework. It had a balustrade around it that I used as a ladder to climb up and have a look at the top of the pagoda. I nearly fell off my makeshift ladder in fright when huge bats flew out at me, looking like horrible foxes with wings, but when I'd recovered my nerve I peered into the top of the pagoda. Right up high was a coffin, but when I investigated further there was no one in it.

My men and I chatted about the mystery of the empty coffin while we set to work cleaning up the damage. It seemed the right thing to do.

'I suppose the Japanese made this mess,' commented Dhanaphal.

'I can't think who else would have done this,' I said.

'We have company,' said Lurdu Swami, glancing towards the windows.

I looked around and noticed a group of Burmese people who had gathered to watch us work. I smiled at them and Lurdu Swami gave them a small wave. They smiled back, clearly pleased with our efforts. We were visitors in the country, and I always wanted to be respectful of them and their culture.

We went back to talking about the empty coffin, but it was only later, when we were leaving, that Dhanaphal noticed a coloured carving of a monk in the garden the same size as the coffin.

'How unusual,' said Lurdu Swami.

'Yes – and look at the bells,' said Nagarajan, turning away from the carving.

I followed his gaze and took note of the many bells outside the temple, all made of bronze. Suddenly the breeze came up, causing the hairs on the back of my neck to stiffen. A shadowy figure appeared by the main bell. I noticed the sun was beginning to set. The monk bowed low to us and then used a large hammer to strike the main bell. The noise of temple bells filled the air, their music eerie and somewhat otherworldly. I nodded towards the monk and then we turned to go.

'What a curious place,' said Lurdu Swami as we disappeared into the jungle and began our walk back to base.

Curious indeed.

Chapter 21
Naba, Tinsukia and Shillong
Dec 1944

On December 10, 1944, I celebrated my twenty-third birthday in a small village near Naba in the midst of the Burmese jungle. I don't remember it being much of celebration, as I was very ill, feeling feverish and shaky. All I remember is that I decided to shave my moustache off. I had grown it to appear older because I didn't want members of my team to feel that they were being told what to do by someone who looked like a schoolboy – but now I felt like a change.

I was still feeling awful some days later, and I think we were all struggling to keep our spirits up after being in the jungle for so long, struggling to survive day to day and still do our work, so the decision came from General Festing that we would return to our base workshop in Tinsukia. We flew without incident to Dibrugarh and then drove the rest of the way there. The team I had left there were doing a wonderful job, and it was good to see my men working so efficiently in their air-conditioned workshop. My team of five Indian men were happy to be back for the time being too and immediately slipped back into the rhythms of the larger team. We hoped to be back to Burma as soon as I was well enough, but my health continued to worsen. I had a high temperature and was also running to the toilet constantly.

For some time, I had been telling my men that I would eat the same food that they did, so they spiced the food we had Indian-style. At first it was very tasty, but I noticed as time went on the food was getting hotter and hotter. I wondered if they were waiting for me to admit that I couldn't eat it. I was too stubborn to admit that, but that ended up being part of my undoing. In terrible pain and feeling weak, I was examined by an army doctor, and he told me I had damaged my stomach lining with all the extra-spicy food. I had severe dysentery and it was also confirmed that I had malaria. I was ordered to Shillong for medical treatment.

I landed in Shillong just before Christmas feeling the most ill I have ever felt. To make matters worse, I was well aware that the drive from the airfield to the hospital was terribly dangerous. I remember lying there feeling desperately ill, the grinding noise of the gears of the army trucks splitting my head with the terrible noise they made going up the steep mountains. The roads were only half an inch wider than the truck I was travelling in with other ill men – a truck being used as an ambulance – and we were up three thousand feet and the cliffs went straight down.

'Don't look,' warned the driver.

He drove scraping the side of his vehicle against the cliff edge. Later, when I was recovering, I heard a story that one of the trucks had gone over the edge after hitting a pothole, the driver having lost control. Eleven men had plummeted to their deaths.

We finally arrived in Shillong, and I got the medical treatment I needed and had a long period of rest. I really don't remember much about my second visit to this beautiful area, as I was so unwell during this time. The only thing I can remember is that they made me drink a glass of quinine each day, which was a horrible-tasting fluid. Everything else is a blur.

Chapter 22
Katha
Jan 1945

Weeks later I was finally well again, so my five Indians and I returned to Burma. The first night we arrived, the wind was blowing hard, and, unfortunately, our tent had no walls. I spend the night in wet clothes and worried that my good health wouldn't last very long in these trying conditions, but in the morning we organised more substantial accommodation in the village and settled down to our familiar work routine.

Our new base in Katha was near the Irrawaddy River, Burma's largest river, which was over two thousand kilometres long. Navigation on the river was difficult for large vessels because of the numerous sandbanks and islands. It was a wide, dirty river.

We'd only been in Katha a couple of days when I adopted a dog. We'd put up a small tent to keep the sun off us while we were eating and a bitch came looking for scraps. She was a wild dog, but obviously desperate for food to come so close to us. I gave her some food, and, observing her, I guessed that she was probably feeding some pups. Keeping my distance, I followed her into the bush and found where her pups were hidden. I decided that it would be good to have a dog, so I chose the biggest and healthiest looking of the three pups. He was a short-haired, golden-coloured dog that looked a little like a dingo, and he immediately took to me. I named him Lucky, not that I ever called him – with so many Japanese around, that would have been foolish.

Lucky behaved like any other decent dog. He was intelligent and very loyal. He didn't like the Japanese who were making a nuisance of themselves in the area – and he would always growl if a stranger approached us. He used to join me in my slit trench at night and keep watch. He was the sort of dog that every soldier should have, and he was very popular with my team.

Unfortunately, we got orders to cross the Irrawaddy River a few weeks later and I couldn't find him when it came time to go. Lucky often used to disappear into the jungle to hunt rabbits or birds. We had to load our trucks onto rafts, and even though we were the last to load our truck, he didn't turn up in time, so we had to leave him behind. I was ever so sad to lose him, but consoled myself that he was an active, friendly dog, so he would probably be okay and someone else would adopt him – or, at the very least, he would be able to hunt for himself.

On the other side of the Irrawaddy River, we came across a sandy area with lots of thorn bushes and set up camp there. The thorns were so sharp I used them for needles on my gramophone. We found two disused railway trucks that had been used for transporting goods, so we cut windows in them and turned them into workshops.

We were just relaxing after work one day when we noticed two hares hiding in the bushes.

'Rabbit pie would be good,' said Kesavan wistfully.

'I'm so sick of bully beef,' said Nagarajan. 'We've been eating bully beef three times a day forever.'

'It doesn't seem to matter what they do with it, fried or boiled or spiced, it still tastes like bully beef,' said Kesavan. 'I've had enough.'

'We'll let's get those hares, then,' said Nagarajan.

'Good idea,' I said.

We couldn't waste our own ammunition on something so frivolous, but we had several Japanese rifles and some of their shells, so we started firing at the two hares. But we were hopeless shots with the enemy's rifles, and the hares just hopped from thorn bush to thorn bush in response to our feeble attempts.

We were firing and becoming increasingly frustrated when a voice suddenly shouted out in English.

'Stop firing!'

We turned to find an Englishman, dressed in civilian European clothes. We got talking and discovered he was a retired British army soldier who had decided to stay in Burma and who had married a Burmese woman. He was in charge of the local village.

'What are you trying to do?' he asked after introductions had been made.

I gestured toward the two hares. 'We were just hoping for some different food to eat, like rabbit pie.'

He nodded and talked to a couple of local Burmese men who had gathered to see what was going on. In no time at all, these men had used poles with fishing hooks to capture the two hares alive, and they brought them to us. But when I looked at their faces, I suddenly felt very ashamed. The Burmese didn't believe in killing anything, and I could see that these men didn't want to kill the two rabbits, even if they had been asked to.

I looked at my men and saw they were looking as uncomfortable as I was.

I shook my head. 'We've changed our minds,' I said.

'We don't feel like rabbit pie anymore,' said Nagarajan.

'Let them go,' said Kesavan.

'We are so sorry about this,' I said. 'Very, very sorry.'

The Burmese men looked relieved and happy when the Englishman in charge explained we had changed our minds, and the hares quickly scurried away. Their lucky day!

Chapter 23
Bahe
Feb 1945

In February, we caught up with the rest of our division in Bahe, and when we arrived, I discovered General Festing in deep conversation with Lord Louis Mountbatten, who was in overall charge of everything. The general waved me over as they continued talking. They were discussing the problem of crossing the Irrawaddy River at this particular junction and the ongoing problems the Japanese were causing for them in that area as they controlled the nearby island. I listened closely to their conversation. This was the first time I had met Lord Louis Mountbatten. He was a tall, handsome man. He had an aristocratic manner, but as I listened to their discussion it seemed he also had a lot of common sense.

'Every time we try to cross this river, we end up losing good men,' Lord Louis Mountbatten was saying. 'We really have to find a solution.'

'What do you think we should do, Hennessy?' asked General Festing, turning to me.

'I think you should photograph the area,' I said immediately.

'And how would we do that?' asked Lord Louis Mountbatten,

looking at me with interest.

'The Americans have a light plane they use for picking up wounded and taking them to hospital. I've got several working cameras. If we got up there, I could take aerial photographs that could be helpful in identifying enemy positions.'

It never occurred to me to feel shy about speaking freely about my ideas, and my suggestions were greeted with a great deal of enthusiasm. They welcomed the news that I had some working cameras – no mean feat in the Burmese humidity – and in no time at all we had found a twenty-four-year-old American pilot who was keen to take me up. Like the previous American pilots I had met, he was keen to earn more points so he could go home.

We discussed the mission. The cockpit of his plane had a clear plastic cover over the seats so the pilot would do barrel rolls and spend much of his time flying upside down so I could take photographs low over Japanese lines. We worked out how to tie me in so I would have my hands free to take photographs, and I readied the camera. It was going to be dangerous, but I was excited to have the chance to do something so daring!

February 9 was fine and clear, and I didn't feel nervous when we took off, although I did get butterflies in my stomach the first time the pilot rolled the plane! It was exhilarating flying so low upside down over enemy positions, but I somehow managed to keep my hands steady as I shot photographs of the area. From the sky and through a camera lens, it quickly became obvious what the Japanese were up to. The island they apparently controlled had been bombed to smithereens, but they now occupied the southern side of the bank and had obviously tunnelled into the riverbanks. The Irrawaddy River was very dirty, but we could see that they had built a bridge just below the surface of the river so they could run out from their tunnels, fire at will and then simply run back – as though they were walking on water!

The only Japanese we saw during our flight was a solitary soldier. He was standing with his back to a tree and seemed to be laughing, as though it was funny to see us flying upside down. Thankfully, he didn't fire at us, and twenty minutes later we were back on the ground.

After we landed, I handed the films over to the Americans to develop. Sadly, I never saw the photographs myself, but they proved to be extremely helpful and the order came to bomb the newly discovered Japanese positions.

At that point, things became desperate for the Japanese in the area. It was clear those who had survived the bombing were running short of ammunition, food and medical supplies.

Dreadfully, word came back from front-line troops that Japanese troops were being forced up trees to shoot at us, with no hope of coming down from the trees alive. As soon as someone spotted them, they were killed. My men and I continued to do our work, but even though I was pleased that the war was going our way, I was alarmed by the savage loss of life that was occurring. When would the killing end?

About ten days after I had gone up to take photographs, I met some American soldiers who had a brand new Jeep that wasn't working. We got talking. Like all American soldiers, they weren't allowed to drink any hard alcohol; they could drink beer but nothing stronger. Now, because of my rank, I had three bottles of Indian-issued gin in my possession, which they soon noted. (Originally, I had been issued with a bottle of gin, a bottle of whiskey and a bottle of rum – but no one in the British Army wanted the gin we had, so that is how I ended up with three bottles of gin after swapping.) The American soldiers had a cardboard box with thirty-six cans of American beer, which they pulled out of the back of their Jeep.

'Do you want to swap our beer for your gin?' they asked.

'I don't drink alcohol,' I said.

'Oh, so what do you want for your gin?' they asked.

'I'll have the Jeep,' I said, as a joke.

No one was more surprised than me when they agreed! We swapped my gin for their Jeep, and they helped me push it to our base camp. I was fairly confident that it only needed some simple repairs to get it working again. My workshop staff had a look at it and quickly decided that it needed a new engine. It turned out the Americans had been running the engine with no oil in it, so it had seized up. But although we were in the middle of the jungle, getting a new engine didn't end up being a problem! I got my right-hand man Bill, back in our Tinsukia base, onto the job. He organised to get a new engine for General Festing's vehicle parachuted in, and we just took the old engine from the general's Jeep. When my staff were done, my Jeep even had a handbrake and windscreen cushions, and it was the best Jeep in the brigade! It only took a couple of days to organise everything. Once again, I reflected that in the British Army, we repaired everything – in the American Army, they dumped things and waited for new replacements.

To celebrate our new Jeep, we loaded the vehicle with as many men as we could and went to the movie that the Americans were playing that night. It was a rare treat. The Americans regularly had movie screenings, while we never watched anything, so it was an unusual escape into a fictional world away from the Burmese jungle.

I never saw the men I bought the Jeep from again. I don't think they would have got into trouble, however – they could easily 'lose' a Jeep in a railway crash, as they often used Jeeps to pull trains then. They would attach some timber on the front and back to absorb the contact with the trains, but in a crash, the poor Jeeps were squashed to the size of their engines.

I quickly became very attached to my new Jeep. It was really my pride and joy for some time – a rare modern pleasure deep in a sometimes savage and primitive jungle.

Chapter 24
Bahe and Mongmit
Mar 1945

In March, the weather was still hot but thankfully without rain, and we continued to travel from village to village repairing the army instruments as we went. The general always instructed his staff to select areas for us that were relatively safe, as we were a small group of men who were not well armed, but we weren't far from Bahe when we found ourselves in a spot of trouble.

Hoping to buy some eggs, we entered a small village and were just exploring the area to see if we should stay when one of the local men came out to greet us. He was very agitated, and at first we couldn't understand what he was saying because he was so upset, but we found he spoke good English. By that stage we all knew a little Burmese, so we communicated with a mixture of the two languages. It took a while to get the full story, but eventually we learnt some rogue Chinese soldiers had come into the village a few days before, killed and wounded some of the villagers and taken some of their livestock. They were now, understandably, very nervous of strangers.

We assured the man that we were friendly and asked if we could do anything to help. He led us into a bamboo building where there were several wounded people, and we gave them some of our medical supplies. We were talking to another man, who was nursing a wounded arm, when there was a commotion outside – angry voices and women crying and screaming.

I glanced at my men and we loaded our weapons. The villager told me the soldiers who had been killing and looting had returned. We went outside determined to protect the Burmese, and there we witnessed Chinese soldiers rounding up the village goats and chickens.

'You can't take our livestock,' one of the Burmese men was shouting. 'They are all we have.'

Several of the women were wailing.

I quickly surveyed the situation. There were fifteen American-supported Chinese soldiers, and they looked well fed, well clothed and well armed. They were clearly the soldiers who had caused problems in the first place, a band of men who were separated from their main unit and who were acting like common criminals.

I turned to my men. 'Point your weapons at them and prepare to fire,' I said in a loud voice so that everyone would hear me.

My men did as I asked, although I noticed that Nagarajan's hands were shaking just a little. He was an intelligent lad and he would have immediately noticed what I did. We were outmanned, and, more problematically, we were completely outgunned. All I had on my person was a Sten gun, which was a very ordinary weapon, and my Indians had rifles that were positively ancient. The Chinese had American machine guns, the very latest of weapons. They raised their weapons at us as the villagers began to back away from the developing scene. This was a risky bluff, hoping the Chinese might think we had more weapons than we did.

'Get out of this village!' I shouted at the Chinese man closest to me.

There was a flicker in his eye, so I thought he probably understood what I had said. A lot of the Chinese I had met could understand some English, and even if they couldn't, I would think our intention was clear. We wanted them to leave. I noticed him looking at my uniform.

'Get out!' I said again.

We continued to stand with our weapons pointed at each other, and I could feel sweat on my forehead as the minutes began to tick by. I was aware that if they opened fire we were dead men, but I felt surprisingly calm.

'You leave this village now and don't come back,' I said. 'Otherwise I'm going to cause you a lot of trouble.'

My mind was racing. We were supposed to be on the same side! If they did shoot us, they would be in enormous trouble, and the Burmese people were here to witness it all. Would they risk shooting British and Indian Army soldiers just for the sake of a few chickens and goats? But then again, where was law and order in the middle of the jungle and in the middle of war? They could kill everyone and no one might ever know.

The minutes stretched as we continued to train our weapons on these renegade Chinese soldiers. The insects droned in the background, and the sun beat down on us relentlessly as we stood like statues in our Mexican standoff, each of us waiting for the other to make the first move. It seemed like we had been standing there for hours, but it was probably only ten minutes before the Chinese soldier closest to me slowly lowered his weapon and began to step backwards and away from our group. The other Chinese soldiers followed his lead. We kept our weapons on them until they had disappeared from sight, their heads bowed because they had lost face. I didn't think they would be back to bother this village again.

When they were gone, we put away our weapons. Nagarajan wiped his forehead with the back of his hand, Kesavan audibly sighed with relief and I felt dizzy as adrenalin surged through me. Then another commotion broke out as the Burmese people descended on us, laughing and crying, patting our backs and thanking us in loud voices.

They treated us like we were heroes, but I considered the fact that Allied troops had been causing problems in the first place outrageous. The Burmese were clearly pleased that we had got rid of the rogue soldiers threatening them and their livestock, but that wasn't going to bring back their dead or help their wounded. But I was once again pleased with my men. They had followed my orders without question, and we had stood our ground together. I was very proud of them – this situation was well and truly beyond what would normally be expected of army instrument repairers.

Later we found ourselves off-road, following horse tracks with the smell of fresh manure. At this point I didn't know where we were; I was just conscious we should be heading south.

We were travelling in the middle of dense jungle when Lurdu Swami pointed out a curious sight. There was a small building constructed of corrugated iron that had a square lawn in front of it.

'I don't like the look of this,' I said.

'Who would create a lawn in the middle of the jungle?' asked Dhanaphal.

'Japanese?' asked Ngarajan.

We parked some distance out of sight and crept through the

jungle so we could better see the building. It was only the size of a small hut but looked in such good condition I considered that someone must be using it, especially as I could smell very fresh horse manure. I noticed tracks leading to an underground stable near to the main building, but it was empty.

The lawn was immaculately groomed, and it flashed through my head that the Japanese probably liked beheading people in such a setting. I forced this thought away and told my men to take positions in the jungle around the building so they could provide me with cover. This definitely needed investigating.

'I think there's someone in there,' I said. 'I'll run into the building from the back. Wait for me to come out the front and keep your guns ready to fire, whatever happens.'

I inched around to the back of the building, peeking through the window as I did so. I could see a Japanese officer sitting on a chair. I could tell he was an officer from the uniform he was wearing – and since he was an officer, I had no choice but to take offensive action. The officers were responsible for a lot of our soldiers being killed, so he couldn't be left to his own devices. Our small team wasn't equipped to take prisoners, so I entered the building firing my Sten gun.

Everything seemed to happen in slow motion. The officer turned towards me as I entered the building and then fell to the floor, his mouth open in surprise from having been shot. My heart was pounding as I looked around. The only thing in the room was a chair and a table with a small, half-finished plate of food on it. I had obviously come in when he was eating and surprised him. I looked at him for a moment. I didn't feel guilty about shooting him; if anything, I just felt curious that he was there on his own.

I went out to talk to my men. I decided that we would be best to hide the body, so we dragged the officer into the jungle under some bushes and covered him up. It seemed wise to quickly leave the area, so we hurriedly made our way back to the Jeep and sped off. I didn't want to hang around to see if other Japanese came to investigate. That would be asking for trouble.

We finally got our bearings and spent that night at Mongmit. In the morning, we were working on repairing some binoculars when a dealer approached us selling jewels. The area we were in was rocky and hilly, and although I never saw the jewel mines, I had heard about them. I watched the dealer with interest as he opened the small suitcase that he carried. He was Burmese but spoke good English, and he made a big song and dance about each of the jewels that he presented. The trays in his case were filled with glittering jewels, mainly rubies but also some amethysts and sapphires.

Many of the soldiers with me didn't believe these jewels were real – but I had microscopes and I could easily check if the gems were real or machine-made. Some of the soldiers bought jewels for their sweethearts back home.

I ended up buying a selection. Burmese jewels are some of the most beautiful in the world. It was the first time I had seen star rubies and star sapphires, which have a six-legged star in the middle of the jewel. I didn't know it at the time, but these jewels that I bought for a shilling or two each are highly sought after by jewel experts, and these days are worth at least five thousand US dollars per carat. From then on, I was travelling with a bag of uncut jewels worth a small fortune in my personal effects.

Chapter 25
Mong Long and Mandalay
Apr 1945

Our time in Mong Long was relatively uneventful, and in April we departed, our next destination Mandalay. This was extremely rugged terrain, and we had to go through the Gokteik Gorge following rough jungle tracks that zigzagged up and down steep, rocky mountains. When we got to the bottom of the gorge, we had to cross a small river. The original bridge had been blown up, but thankfully our engineers had constructed a temporary bridge for us to cross the river, although I felt relieved when we were finally on the other side. We travelled in convoy with our two three-tonne trucks and Jeep.

We had spent several days travelling, the landscape rocky, bleak and eventually monotonous, when two lizards ran across the road in front of our Jeep. They were so colourful I slowed to have a look. One was blue and one was an orange-gold colour. They didn't look real. They were so shiny and bright they looked like they were made of metal.

We came to crossroads and there was a group of Gurkhas, Nepalese soldiers who, in the Indian and British Armies, were renowned for their bravery and courage. There were dead

Japanese all over the road, and the Gurkhas nodded at us grimly as we passed by. It was another reminder that the war was not yet over.

Mandalay was a relatively big town, and we had a lot of work on our plate to get through while we were based there. I met a family who were of mixed Burmese-British descent, and my men and I ended up having a number of meals with them. The father was an experienced watchmaker, and he showed me some wonderful examples of beautiful watches that he had expertly repaired. We had a lot in common and I thoroughly enjoyed our conversations. He was extremely clever and had made tools to do his work from a crashed British plane. I gave him some of my files when I saw he didn't have any.

During this period, I was repairing a lot of watches, but this work often filled me with great sadness. The Japanese had captured many islands during the war; they had killed a lot of men and often kept their watches. But now many Japanese were being killed, and it wasn't uncommon for Chinese soldiers to take these watches from their corpses and then bring them to me for repair. Very often I would discover they were engraved and were some New Zealander's or Australian's twenty-first birthday present. It still makes me feel sad that so many of these young men died and probably never had much of a chance against the well-trained Japanese and their superior weapons earlier on in the war.

However, I was never anti-Japanese, despite everything that I saw. I just viewed them as individuals, and I actually admired them often, as they showed so much common sense. Sometimes I came across Japanese soldiers who were wounded and who could speak English. My men and I always gave those men cigarettes and chocolate if we had them. Admittedly, some of them spoke fanatically about how they were sure they would win the war, even though things were desperate for them in Burma, but they didn't have much to say when I said, 'There's no show as you don't have the numbers.'

But many of them talked sensibly. There was one young Japanese soldier I met who had been a salesman in New York and London prior to the war. He said the only reason he had joined the Japanese Army because he was in Japan at the time and they were rounding up all the young men. He didn't have a choice.

'How can a small country like Japan beat America and everyone else?' he said. 'I've seen America; I've seen England. Japan can't possibly win this war.'

In the middle of a tiny village, we met another Japanese soldier who had married a Burmese girl. He'd run away from the Japanese Army after stealing items from their stores. He'd put the stolen goods on a horse with his wife, and he'd travelled until he found the village where the young woman had grown up and still had family. The family took them both in, and he gave them the stolen goods in return for looking after his wife if he ever got captured or killed. After that, he kept his head down, hoping to keep out of trouble. He looked alarmed when he saw us and immediately put his arms up and offered to surrender to us, but we couldn't take any prisoners – we weren't equipped to do this – so we just told him to stay put and keep out of trouble. He'd been working in his garden and was wearing civilian clothes and didn't look like a threat to anyone.

'I'll be pleased when all this silly fighting is over,' he said. 'Then I can just settle down and live a normal life with the woman I love.'

The Burmese people who became our friends in Mandalay were completely pro-British but very supportive of one Japanese soldier they had met, who was a talented artist. They showed us his photograph several times and asked if we ever encountered him that we not shoot him but lock him up instead so he would survive the war. He was an officer in the area who was respected by a number of people, as he was very kind to everyone, whereas many of the Japanese were cruel. We never ran into him, and I hope he survived. But at that stage of the war, I don't know how good his odds would have been of survival. The Japanese were dying in their thousands, from malaria, from the lack of medicine, from the lack of food.

The Burmese family was very attractive and extremely hospitable and welcoming. The only time I saw them upset was when they spotted a black-and-yellow centipede that was about ten inches long. Their daughter screamed loudly, and it was clear they were all very scared of the insect. They told me a centipede's poison was worse than a snake's, and I had no reason not to believe them. I was very sad when we had orders to leave Mandalay. Gabriel, however, was much sadder than me – I found out later that he was quite attracted to their vivacious, pretty daughter. He was depressed for several weeks afterwards and quite unlike his usual self.

Chapter 26
Meiktila
May 1945

Despite the beginning of the monsoon season and the incessant rain, we travelled south to Meiktila, and there was an increasing feeling of exhilaration that the war in Europe would be over soon. On our travels we met an old Burmese man who lived in a tiny house and who represented, in many ways, the thoughts of a lot of people at that time, even the locals. When he saw us travelling, he came out to meet us and stood to attention, saluting us like a British soldier would. We stopped to talk to him.

'God bless the King,' he said to us in excellent English.

'How do you come to speak such good English?' I asked.

'I'm a schoolteacher,' he replied. 'And I'm pleased that the Germans will be defeated soon. And then everyone can concentrate on the Japanese and get them out of Burma.'

I couldn't agree with his sentiments more, and each day we listened to the news coming through with growing interest, although we worked as hard as ever repairing instruments.

When we arrived in Meiktila, I discovered that General Festing was severely ill with malaria and he had been transported to a hospital in Poona. A temporary officer had been put in charge, a captain of mixed race – part Indian, part English.

I first discovered him in an office going through piles of documents, and I immediately thought he looked shifty. My first impressions were confirmed when he ordered me across town to pick up some watches he needed repaired. When I came back from this errand, I discovered that my Jeep had disappeared. When I investigated further, I learnt that the new officer had sold my Jeep! I realise I'd never officially owned it – it was actually owned by the Americans – but I considered it mine, and I was furious that this upstart who hadn't seen anything of war had stolen it from me. There was nothing I could do, but I was incredibly angry that he'd sold it and probably pocketed the money for himself. It was on our inventory, so I guess he saw his chance to make some cash.

I was even angrier when I saw him several days later using some of our correspondence for bookmarks. I suspect he was up to no good in many ways. Several people mentioned to me that he appeared to be falsifying paperwork and changing who was recommended for medals. I didn't see this myself, but it wouldn't have surprised me.

On May 8 we got the news about VE Day in Europe – the war there was finally over. It is hard to describe our jubilation! I was very thrilled, and even though our war was still going, it didn't seem it would be long before the Japanese would be defeated too.

American crews arrived into Burma that day to take us back to India. The scenes in Burma were chaotic, with men moving in all directions. It was a very happy day, but also sad in hindsight as that was the last time I saw my fine Indian men who had been

Meiktila   *May 1945*

with me on my adventures in the Burmese jungle. They were heading back on a separate transport from me, but I found each of them and shook their hands before they left. We didn't say much, but the moment was poignant. Lurdu Swami patted me on the back when he shook my hand. Dhanaphal couldn't stop smiling, while Gabriel politely thanked me for being in charge of them. Nagarajan looked quite emotional, while Kesavan showed his feelings by thumping me on the shoulder. Their faces said it all. They were clearly proud to have served in our unit, to have contributed to the war efforts with their considerable skills, and they were pleased to be going home – but, like me, they were also sad that our adventure was ending.

When I got to my allocated plane, there was a large group of men waiting to board. We were told by the Americans that we weren't allowed to take everything with us, as the planes were overloaded. I had to leave behind our rifles and ammunition – everything we could be seen to be carrying. I also had to leave behind all my instruments and repair equipment. At that stage I had about four hundred watches that only needed simple repairs, but I just had to leave them to disintegrate in the jungle.

Despite this setback, the feeling of elation was infectious, and some soldiers, including me, gave the Americans some of our jewels. I had a small tobacco tin, and I removed the cigarettes, put some jewels in them and put them in my shorts pocket after giving some to the crew. The rest of the jewels I buried, like many other men, but I doubt anyone would have much hope of finding them again. I imagine there are bundles of jewels still hidden in the dense Burmese jungle, the spots they had been buried covered in native plants. The jewels were worth a lot of money, but I just thought, 'What if the plane crashes because people are being greedy and taking too many things?'

I looked down on the dense canopy of jungle as we flew out of Burma, and I couldn't help smiling. The relatively civilized streets of Poona beckoned, and the war was nearly over. I counted myself a lucky man.

Chapter 27
Poona, Rangoon and Nashik
Jun – Sep 1945

Unfortunately, I hadn't been in Poona very long when I had to go to hospital again. I had a temperature of 103 degrees, and I was once more plagued with malaria. Even though I've always been a slight fellow, after being ill this time I only weighed eight stone. But by August I was back in Burma, this time on my own, doing instrument repairs.

I was based near Rangoon, the capital of Burma, when the news came that the US had dropped the atomic bomb on Hiroshima on August 6, and then several days later they dropped another on Nagasaki. When the news came over British radios that the Japanese had surrendered on August 15, there was a great deal of celebration – until it became clear that the Japanese in Burma didn't know of the surrender. Many of them had no working radios, and the few that did refused to believe that the Emperor of Japan had surrendered. To them it was inconceivable.

The fighting in Burma continued in earnest until brave officers from the 36th Indian Division volunteered to go to local Japanese in our area with British radios so they could contact their commanders and learn the news firsthand. The officers arranged this through Burmese people who were in contact with the Japanese. It was a very strange time. The war was officially over, but men on both sides were still fighting. Finally, the Japanese in the area accepted they had lost the war, and they began to retreat. There was no need for me to remain in Burma, so I headed back to India once more.

It was a jubilant time from then on. Words can't describe the elation that everyone felt that finally the madness had ended! I remember being back in India and walking the streets marvelling that all my team had somehow survived the war and we could now get on with the next stage of our lives. Many of the Englishmen in my unit were already getting on ships to go back home, including Bill, my right-hand man, who had done such a fine job for me organising all the paperwork for whatever equipment we needed. He was in high spirits the last time I saw him, eager to get back home and return to civilian life. We all felt the same, and I know my letters to my family back home reflected my excitement.

I was due to return home myself when I was laid low with malaria and severe dysentery again and was back in hospital, this time in Nashik, so once again the course of my experience of war was forever altered. By the time I got out, everyone I knew had gone and I'd had another idea. I had heard over the radio that occupation troops were preparing to go to Japan. I decided it would be interesting to go and have a look for myself before I finally went home. So I reported to the nearest authority with as much confidence as I could muster and explained I had been in hospital but was now ready for active duty again. There were no checks, and, in all the confusion and chaos of men arriving and departing, I was easily able to attach myself to a new unit of men arriving from England. All I had to do was produce my paybook; it was really that simple.

I thought to myself, 'I've come a long way, and this is my chance to see more of the world and get paid for it.'

Chapter 28
Nashik and Bombay
Oct 1945 – Mar 1946

I hadn't had any leave during my time in Burma, so I had some time off before departing for Japan. I spent my time teaching photography to some of the Gurkha officers, and we discovered that the best time of the day to develop films was at two in the morning, as that was the coolest time of the night. I also explored the temples of Nashik and took many photographs for my own enjoyment.

Preparing for Japan, they gave us new uniforms to wear and we were told that we needed to be smarter than before. We all shaved regularly, for one thing! I enjoyed meeting the people from the new unit, although I felt sad that I wasn't working with my wonderful Indian men. They had all gone back to their homes, and I hoped I might see them again one day in the future. But my new unit were all happy to have a technical person on their team, and I probably made myself welcome by repairing their watches and other personal effects. We didn't have much in the way of training, however, not even any lessons in Japanese, but no one was bothered about the lack of preparation. It was a very happy, somewhat chaotic time.

By Christmas 1945 there were a lot of new people in town, and the atmosphere was like a non-stop party, although sometimes all the excessive revelry got out of hand. We had a wonderful celebration on Christmas Day while we were stationed in Nashik. The Second Brigade, which was part of the Commonwealth Brigade, was celebrating the end of the war and our impending trip to Japan with gusto. Unfortunately, when doing a drunken conga line through the mess tent, they knocked over the oil lamps and the tent caught alight. Everyone got out in one piece, but then I had to rescue two officers who were so drunk that they fell into the monsoon trenches. Needless to say, as the only non-drinker in the group, I was the only one with a clear head the next morning.

Before going to Japan, I spent some time in Bombay and met Lionel, my younger brother, there. He had recently turned eighteen and was studying to be an officer, and he was staying with about twelve other men in a hotel. It was wonderful to see him after all those years overseas, although the first thing I noticed was that he was now much taller than me!

Lionel was in India in the role of a military policeman, which wasn't a popular position, but he did a really good job, especially in stopping our men going to the local brothels. The brothels in Bombay were terrible. There was an entire street where women whose husbands had been killed, and who usually had children to feed, had turned to prostitution to support themselves. They were housed in rooms with bars, just like cages, and the risk of disease was incredibly high. So Lionel turned his attention to the brothels and arrested every soldier who went near this notorious street – and no doubt ended up saving many soldiers from terrible diseases, even if they didn't appreciate what he had done for them at the time!

I thoroughly enjoyed spending time with my brother, but it wasn't long before I had to join up with my new unit, as we were ready to ship to Japan.

Chapter 29
Kure and Hiroshima
Apr – Jun 1946

My new unit travelled to Japan via Singapore. When we first arrived in Japan, it was snowing, so that was a shock to my system after so long experiencing tropical heat. The British Commonwealth Occupation Force Headquarters was in Kure, about twenty miles from Hiroshima. The area around Kure was extremely mountainous, but Kure itself was flat. Kure had been famous for building *Yamato*, the world's largest battleship, but when I saw their docks they were completely devastated. There were all these warships that had been sunk, but the water was so shallow they were all standing up at odd angles and the wrecks were clearly visible. It was now a graveyard for the remains of many of the Imperial Japanese Navy battleships. It was a strange, eerie sight.

The Americans were in charge of the occupation forces in Japan, but I didn't see any Americans where we were. There were a number of British, Indian, Australian and New Zealander troops in Kure, and we were all housed together in very basic accommodation. We had barracks where we bunked four to a tiny room, with mattresses that were made of an inch of horse hair and as hard as rock. We had electricity, but all the electric wires were bare, without any insulation. The Americans simply nailed cotton reels through the wires to stop them connecting and shorting, admittedly a very economical way to provide us with power. There was a single passage in the barracks so the sergeant major could walk along and easily see us in each of the rooms.

The first thing we did after we had unpacked our gear was explore Kure. It appeared to be a bombed-out ghost town. There were no Japanese people to be seen. Then I decided that I should go and look at Hiroshima, so I borrowed a truck and drove to the devastated city. Being an independent person, I was keen to see with my own eyes what the city looked like after having an atomic bomb dropped on it. The newspaper reports talked about everything being blasted to pieces and said that you could see shadows of people who had been vaporised on the walls. I wondered if things had been exaggerated.

I visited Hiroshima in April 1946, so that was some eight months after the atomic bomb had been dropped, and it was clear that the devastation was immense. There really was nothing left around ground zero, a roughly circular area of around four square miles – just piles of rubble. And even outside that area, there were no wooden buildings left; they had all burned down. I saw glass that had probably been separate sheets that had melted into a single block. And I saw people who were in a terrible state, even after having had medical treatment. The devastation was terrible and undeniable.

But I also notice there were green shoots sprouting from the burnt trees, and where there had been concrete framework, it was still standing, although some was cracked in places. I noticed that in buildings, taps were still intact. I didn't see any 'shadows' of the dead, but instead evidence of life. People were returning to Hiroshima, and sawmills were working overtime to create new wooden buildings to house the multitude of people who were now homeless.

Another of the newspaper reports at the time said all the bricks had turned to dust, but that wasn't true. When I left Hiroshima, I took some bricks back with me and put them on the beds of the men I was sharing with. It became quite a discussion point when they found them!

I wasn't worried about possible radiation from my visit. There had been published reports deeming it safe for occupation forces to be in the area, even if you spent eight hours per day for ten months in the worst-affected area.

Back in Kure, the local people were starting to venture out, and it turned out to be a more vibrant city than I had first thought, despite the evidence of heavy bombing and fire damage. The streets began to fill up with people wearing an odd mixture of European and traditional dress. But they were terribly afraid of us to begin with. They honestly thought we were going to line them up against a wall and shoot them!

The occupation forces were there to help, not hinder, however. And I was determined to extend the arm of friendship to any Japanese person I met. The two main objectives of the occupation were to help Japan become a democracy and to eliminate any future war threat. We were also there to ensure Japan didn't starve to death, and soldiers before us had set up a food distribution network. Billions of dollars of aid was pouring into Japan at that time.

Merchants started to appear on the street selling their wares, and the cinema and dance halls began to open. You could buy tickets for dances with the local girls – half the money would go to them and the other half to the people who owned the hall. Quite a lot of the girls could speak English, but at first they wouldn't dance with me. But then I finally got friendly with a lovely young woman, Kazue, and her friend Roze. I used to dance with Kazue, and she agreed to meet me for walks around Kure. All the men in her family had been sent overseas. It was through discussions with her and her friend that I discovered the reason the Japanese women, in particular, were so frightened of us.

'Our soldiers have been away being policemen in other countries,' Kazue said. 'This is in countries that have lost control, so they need our help to maintain order. Our men are very honourable.'

'But we've been told that in Britain and America, to become a sergeant in the army, you have to kill your grandmother – and to become a higher rank, you have to kill your mother,' Roze told me.

They had been completely brainwashed. They had no idea what their soldiers were really doing, they hadn't heard about Pearl Harbour and they honestly believed the Japanese Army hadn't done any harm. But in time they came to see that the Allied forces weren't to be feared, and I ended up having some very interesting discussions with them. They dressed in traditional kimonos one afternoon and let me take photographs of them at a local park.

'I'm very pleased you didn't kill your mother or grandmother,' Kazue said to me in all seriousness.

A number of young women had turned to prostitution, but Kazue only worked at the dance hall and seemed to be making enough to live on – and I always sought her out to dance with her.

I do recall that they only had one band, and they did a terrible job playing European instruments until one of the occupying Indian men, who was a jazz specialist on the trumpet, started giving them lessons. They improved considerably, and it made the difference between music no one could dance to and music that got everyone up on the floor!

One day, I met a smartly dressed young Japanese man and we got talking. He was cleaning cooking pots that had thick charcoal burnt onto them, scrubbing them clean until they were shiny and new. He seemed to be much too intelligent to be doing this menial job.

'What did you do before?' I asked.

'I was the captain of a submarine,' was his reply. I wasn't surprised when he told me this. There was an authority in his bearing that made it completely believable, and I pondered how much everything had changed for him.

Kure was a defeated, sad place in many ways. It was close enough to witness the devastation of Hiroshima – and, by all accounts, the people had valiantly provided much-needed medical aid to many survivors. Then the area had been hit by a deadly typhoon a month later, and more than a thousand people died. Many of the women had lost all their male family members. The people were confused and scared, and life was very tough. Even with all the aid pouring in, many were close to starvation.

I used to regularly see an old man who looked so miserable I wouldn't have been surprised to learn that all his family had been killed during the war. I wanted to cheer him up, so I gave him a tin of sardines. He looked very surprised, and, after that, every time he saw me he bowed low to the ground. Unfortunately, he didn't speak English, so I never found out what his story was.

The bathhouse was very popular with the local people. It was a large building and inside were barrels around a large pool. People would soap themselves up in the barrels and then jump into the main pool to rinse off. They seemed to have separate times when men used the bathhouse and when women and children used them. Needless to say, a lot of soldiers got quite interested, and some were in the habit of trying to peek into the building to get glimpses of the local women naked. I didn't agree with their behaviour – after all, we were the invaders, and we were supposed to be there to help them, not spy on them.

When I was in Japan, I looked at everyone I met and thought, 'What can I do to create goodwill?' We wanted to help them become self-supporting, and I just thought the more goodwill we could show them, the less problems everyone would have in the future.

Back at our barracks, we were having a few problems, however. All the glass windows had fallen out because the stoppers didn't work. And we had a fire caused by soldiers smoking that was thankfully contained. But the worst thing was they had built toilets under the barracks and the stench was terrible. We all complained about it, but oddly enough our waste was part of a plan of improving Japanese agriculture in the area. Every Wednesday afternoon, a horse and trailer with big barrels rode under the building and men collected the waste. Then children were employed to spoon the mixture onto the plants, which were mostly wheat.

I ended up being quite independent when I was in Japan, and I spent a lot of time on my own. I explored the local area very thoroughly, and, one day, up in the hills above the docks, I discovered a large tunnel with drilling equipment. I walked around and saw there were hundreds of machines and they were exact copies of an original drilling machine that I suspected was probably German and Swiss. But, curiously, there was all this equipment but nobody working there – or that's what I thought, until I noticed some boiling water and touched some of the tools to find they were still warm. I strolled out of the tunnel and then snuck back in, and, sure enough, workers had reappeared in that time. They looked at me with a great deal of fear, obviously thinking I was going to shoot them, until I managed to find someone who spoke English and convinced them that I meant no harm, that I was just curious about their operation. After that, they were quite friendly. And they confirmed what I had originally surmised – that they had taken a high-class design and they were now copying it. They were very good at doing that.

I would have loved to have spent more time in Japan at this time after the war, but eventually the authorities discovered I was in the wrong place and I was asked to board a ship to return home. I wasn't in any trouble, and I was pleased I had made it to Japan before going home. After all the fighting in Burma and all that I had seen, I still viewed Japanese as individuals, and I certainly didn't hate them, unlike some of the other soldiers I had met. I didn't hate the Germans, either. I was born in Germany, after all, and knew many Germans who were still my friends, despite the conflict. I wished both countries and their people all the best, and I hoped they would go on to prosper and live in harmony with the rest of the world.

In many ways, I had a different experience of war from many of my contemporaries. Heading up a travelling workshop gave me a different vantage point, and as I used to take a lot of photographs during this time, I was in a position where I spoke to a lot of other people. Rather than placing people in the camp of either 'ally' or 'enemy', I met and spoke to people as individuals and discovered that there were good and bad people on both sides of the war, that the conflict certainly wasn't black or white, and that most people were simply trying to muddle through the insanity as best as they could with the hope that they would survive.

When I look back on my war experience, I don't feel proud or puffed up about anything I did – rather, I feel quietly satisfied that I treated everyone I met with respect. If I was able to help someone then I did, and I was friendly to the people that I met. I feel that I emerged from war the same person, that I wasn't damaged but intact. I consider myself lucky to have survived the global carnage still myself – a reluctant soldier who had to go to war, who only ever wanted peace for everyone.

Final tribute

The following speech was given by Ashok Magan on November 20, 2014 at Brian Hennessy's funeral.

I am honoured to speak today on behalf of the staff of Hennessy Grading Systems, a company which was the brainchild of Brian Hennessy. I would like to give you a perspective of Brian and his work as he was seen, by his staff, his customers and the industry.

I first met Brian at a dinner party in the late nineties, and, since then, I was fortunate enough to also work for him for a few years, recently providing leadership to the business. Brian Hennessy was a scientist, inventor and an innovator. He led change by creating measurement technology which forever changed the way the meat industry operated. The instruments he produced levelled the playing field for farmers so that they could be paid fairly for their efforts. He understood the fundamental principal that you cannot manage anything you can't measure.

Brian achieved world fame twenty-five years ago – the meat industry worldwide recognised the value of his instruments and his insights into using light reflectance to measure meat quality. His inventions earned him fourteen international awards, the most notable being the Prince Phillip Award and the Field Day Awards for Invention and Innovation. His invention was patented in most of the countries the company was operating in. Today the Hennessy Probe is used in more than fifty countries. And they are quality products – even today, the company still receives probes for service manufactured over thirty years ago, and they still continue to function.

Brian was one of the pioneers who established New Zealand as a place of great ideas and creative people. In Europe especially, he enjoyed relationships with governments such as the Netherlands, Germany and in Scandinavia, as they sought ways to improve meat productions and pay farmers fairly based on the quality of their produce. He built a company based on his passion for science. He was inspired by great scientists like Isaac Newton. On his wall in his room, he had photos of the great inventors and photos depicting the moments of discovery these great scientists made. It was always more than just money. It was about pushing the frontiers of science. In fact, there is a sign in the office that says, 'This is a non-profit organisation. It wasn't meant to be, but that's the way it turned out.'

Brian promoted a culture of innovation, and the people who work there enjoy a freedom to develop their potential. Today we call such places 'incubators'. At times, he had twenty-five people working at the company and also an office in Europe. He attracted some of the top brains of the industry to Hennessy. These people went from Hennessy and today have hugely successful businesses in New Zealand. So, on behalf of the staff of Hennessy, Brian, we would like to thank you for the opportunity you provided for the people who worked at Hennessy Grading Systems.

As the news of Brian's passing spread this week, we received some heart-warming messages from people around the world describing how great it was to have worked at Hennessy. I know from conversations with Brian that he would like me to thank the staff at Hennessy who are here today and who have been loyal to him for many years, for example, Heath, who joined Hennessy over thirty years ago. Cho, the principal engineer, has been here for around fifteen years, Anne for over ten years and Ali for seven years. Thank you all for your dedication, for your visits to Brian and always paying him the respect he deserved.

I need to make a special mention of one person at Hennessy who has made a difference to Brian's life – Sarah Hunter. She joined Hennessy twenty-five years ago as an administrator and receptionist, and today she is the managing director. A faithful employee who over time became the stabilising factor for Hennessy and a beacon of hope for Brian. She ensured Brian was prudent in his decisions so that the company continued to operate profitably and maintain the customer base while Brian became less and less involved. Sarah became Brian's ray of sunshine. She used to visit him every day at the rest home and sometimes more than once. He would find excuses and create situations, knowing full well that Sarah would appear soon enough to sort things out. She cared for him, listened to his stories, even when towards the end he was blurring dreams with reality. She built him a garden on his balcony, and birds would come and he would feed them. I know that seeing Sarah daily was his link to his creations of the past and also to fulfil his aspirations for the future, such as writing his memoir.

Sarah did things for Brian which gave him dignity. For example, Sarah used to get Brian's clothes laundered outside the rest home so that they would be better pressed and always looked good. Of course, she never hesitated to put him straight when he needed to be told in no uncertain terms. So Sarah, on behalf of Brian, I would like to take this opportunity to acknowledge your dedication to Brian's success and well-being right up to the very end.

On behalf of Sarah and the staff at Hennessy, we would like to thank the staff at the rest home where Brian lived. That you for your efforts. And especially Patrick Ferryhouse for taking excellent care of Brian.

One last comment. A few months ago, Brian and I were having a light conversation about death. I said to Brian I thought he would live to 101 so that he could get a letter from the Queen. And he replied that he was targeting 102 because his neighbour at home made it to 101, so he had to compete.

So today we say bye to you, Brian.

About the authors

After the war, Brian Hennessy returned home to England, where he married, had three children and opened his own repair business. In 1952, he immigrated to New Zealand with his family, and he served in the New Zealand Army until 1964. He and his wife ran a dairy farm for a number of years, after which he owned a repair shop on Queen St in Auckland.

In 1976, he invented a system of grading meat, and founded Hennessy Grading Systems Limited. This is now the preferred system for grading meat in over fifty countries worldwide, including twenty-one EU member states. Hennessy grading probes are manufactured in New Zealand and supported by service centres around the world, which are managed by Sarah Hunter. Brian died in November 2014, aged ninety-two.

Karen McMillan, who helped Brian with the writing of this book, is the author of both fiction and non-fiction titles, including *The Paris of the East*, *The Paris of the West*, *Unbreakable Spirit*, *Watching Over Me*, *Love Bytes* and *Feast or Famine*. For more information about Karen, visit www.karenm.co.nz.

www.ingramcontent.com/pod-product-compliance
Lightning Source LLC
Chambersburg PA
CBHW051359290426
44108CB00015B/2074